Social Work in the Youth Justice System

Social Work in the Youth Justice System

A MULTIDISCIPLINARY PERSPECTIVE

Darrell Fox and Elaine Arnull

 Open University Press

Open University Press
McGraw-Hill Education
McGraw-Hill House
Shoppenhangers Road
Maidenhead
Berkshire
England
SL6 2QL

email: enquiries@openup.co.uk
world wide web: www.openup.co.uk

and Two Penn Plaza, New York, NY 10121-2289, USA

First published 2013

Copyright © Darrell Fox and Elaine Arnull, 2013

A catalogue record of this book is available from the British Library

ISBN-13: 978-0-33-524569-7 (pb)
ISBN-10: 0-33-524569-2 (pb)
eISBN: 978-0-33-524570-3

Library of Congress Cataloging-in-Publication Data
CIP data applied for

Typesetting and e-book compilations by
RefineCatch Limited, Bungay, Suffolk
Printed and bound by CPI Group (UK) Ltd, Croydon, CR0 4YY

Praise for this book

"This book is an excellent introduction to the important contribution of social workers in the field of work with young offenders. Social work is a key profession in agencies working with such young people, especially in Youth Offending Teams, yet until now it has been a neglected area in social work literature. This will be a key text for social work students and practitioners who need to have an overview of the functions, methods, skills and approaches to working with young offenders."

Brian Littlechild, Professor of Social Work, University of Hertfordshire, UK

"This is a timely book containing much useful information on young people, both as offenders and victims. It covers issues of risk, the scaled approach promoted by the Youth Justice Board, interventions and reflective practice. It will be essential reading for criminology and social work students who should learn about youth justice as well as other professionals in education, police etc. I will be recommending it to my students."

Professor Anthony Goodman, Department of Criminology and Sociology, Middlesex University, UK

"Comprehensive, focused and immediately useful, this book is an articulate and highly readable synthesis of current thinking on social work and a framework to apply this in everyday practice. A refreshing and inspiring view on delinquency and antisocial behaviour. A must have for all the professionals working in the field of juvenile delinquency."

Dalibor Dolezal, Assistant Professor, University of Zagreb, Faculty of Education and Rehabilitation , Sciences, Dept. of Criminology

"Social Work in the Youth Justice System, by Darrell Fox and Elaine Arnull is a welcome analysis and explanation of the tasks and roles which social workers are required to undertake within the Youth Justice system in the UK. Crime and offending by young people in particular are emotive subjects which the media, politicians and the public often feel compelled to share their views on. This book examines in detail the complexities of working as a social worker with young people who offend and will assist prospective and current social workers to negotiate their way through the demanding youth justice environment. The Authors rightly focus on the need for social workers to be creative, ethical and reflective while practicing within a challenging, changing criminal justice setting. The chapters on Assessment, Risk, Legislation and Interventions provide information and analysis which will enable practitioners to understand their roles and be better placed to deliver effective interventions for young people."

David Ellicott, Senior Lecturer, Division of Guidance, Youth Studies and Youth Justice, Nottingham Trent University, UK

Contents

Acknowledgements

We would like to offer our grateful thanks to:

Terry Ann Thomas whose practice knowledge and wisdom has been invaluable in the writing of this book; and Bhavi Teli and others at the YJB who talked with us about current practice and possible future trajectories.

Finally, with love to our families.

Case study

A 14-year-old young woman (J) is arrested for shoplifting a bottle of soft drink priced at £0.75p and receives a reprimand from a police officer at the police station. A short time later the same young women is arrested for the same offence for the same item, again a bottle of soft drink priced at £0.75p. At the police station using the gravity score and the young woman's previous reprimand, the officer is faced with taking no further action or administering a Final Warning and triggering a referral to the Youth Offending Team (YOT) (Crime and Disorder Act 1998, s. 66(1)). This is the case; the girl is referred to the YOT and a Final Warning, Asset assessment and intervention programme are considered. The young person then goes on to shoplift again for yet another bottle of soft drink and as such must be processed speedily through the system and fast-tracked to court. As this is her first offence before the court and for less serious matters for which she has pleaded guilty, she is given a three-month Referral Order.

Abbreviations

AA	Appropriate Adult
ACE	Arts Council of England
ADP	Anti-Discriminatory Practice
AOP	Anti-Oppressive Practice
ASB	Anti-Social Behaviour
Asset	assessment tool
BASW	British Association of Social Work
BME	Black Minority Ethnic
CA	Children Act (denoted by year) 1989 or 2004
CAF	Common Assessment Framework
CAMHS	Child Adolescent Mental Health Service
CBT	Cognitive Behavioural Theory
CDA	Crime and Disorder Act (1998)
CJS	Criminal Justice System (adult)
CPS	Crown Prosecution Service
DCMS	Department of Culture, Media and Sport
DPP	Detention for Public Protection
DTO	Detention Training Order
EBP	Evidence-Based Practice
ECM	Every Child Matters
ETE	education, training and employment
FGC	Family Group Conference
GSCC	General Social Care Council
HCPC	Health and Care Professions Council
ICS	Integrated Children's System
IFP	Intensive Fostering Programme
ISS	Intensive Surveillance and Supervision
ISSP	Intensive Surveillance and Supervision Programme
KEEP	Key Elements of Effective Practice
LD	learning disability/difficulties
LSCB	Local Safeguarding Children Board

MAPPA	Multi-Agency Public Protection Arrangements
NICE	National Institute for Clinical Excellence
NPM	New Public Management
OASys	Offender Assessment System
PACE	Police and Criminal Evidence Act
PAYP	Positive Activities for Young People
PCF	Professional Capabilities Framework
PCR	Post-Court Report
PIF	Placement Information Form
PSR	Pre-Sentence Report
PYO	persistent young offender
RJ	Restorative Justice
RLAA	Remand into Local Authority Accommodation
RNR	Risk, Need and Responsivity
SLA	service-level agreement
SSR	Specific Sentence Report
SWRB	Social Work Reform Board
YISP	Youth Inclusion and Support Programme
VOM	Victim Offender Mediation
VORP	Victim Offender Reconciliation Programme
YJ	youth justice
YJB	Youth Justice Board
YJS	Youth Justice System
YOI	Young Offender Institution
YOP	Youth Offender Panel
YOS	Youth Offending Service
YOT	Youth Offending Team
YRO	Youth Rehabilitation Order

Introduction

The focus of this book is on social work values and how we can find the spaces within youth justice (YJ) practice to uphold and advance these values by working in creative, ethical and reflective ways.

Youth crime is a perennial issue that pervades the media, and young people are often associated with negative images about fear and dangerousness. This pervasive image is now apparently being challenged by the Coalition Government whose initial responses to the riots of 2011 appeared negative, and to highlight young people's involvement, but whose policy paper on 13–19-year-olds is entitled 'Positive for Youth'. The Ministerial Foreword for this document says they are 'passionate about creating a society that is positive for youth . . .' and that '. . . Young people matter. They are important to us now, and to our future, and we need them to flourish . . .' (Department of Education, 2011: Foreword).

The intention appears to be to change the focus from problematic behaviour, to acknowledge the positive behaviour of the majority. It also draws on the language of 'responsibility and respect for others' as well as 'aspiration and pride for themselves.' (Department of Education, 2011: Foreword). Thus although the headline of 'positive' is new, the underlying tenets of the need for inclusion and respect are similar to many of New Labour's social and community foci; for example, the Respect Agenda (1999).

YJ in the UK has, as you will see discussed throughout the book, been an area for debate and contention politically and within academic circles for many years. Since the significant changes to YJ in England and Wales in 1998, it has remained an area of focus, although based on precepts of multidisciplinary, multi-professional work. Social workers practise within the youth justice system (YJS) and as members of multi-agency Youth Offending Teams (YOTs) and bring to it their core values and ethics. As well as understanding and being subject to child welfare legislation, social workers in a YOT must also work within the criminal justice statutes. Age ranges within welfare and justice systems vary and, within the YJS, gender, ethnicity and cultural differences are more pronounced. Interventions are regulated and seek to ensure rehabilitation through accountability with responsibilization, but at all times the welfare of the young person remains paramount. The sometimes competing legal frameworks highlight the complexities of YJ social work as a practice and epitomize the welfare/justice and care/control debates. A practitioner in this setting continually weighs and judges aspects of the young person's welfare against the risk they pose to themselves and society. This makes work in this area challenging, but offers considerable opportunities for creative, reflective and ethical practice: throughout the following chapters we explore how this can be achieved.

1

Welfare and justice: victims and offenders

Before you read this chapter you may want to think about definitions of 'victim' and 'offender' and ask what images these terms create for you?

- Can you think of other terms to use?
- How do you feel about the level of youth crime in this country?
- Do young people who commit crime need help or punishment?
- What is the role of social work with young offenders?

This chapter explores what we know about young people who enter the youth justice system (YJS) and possibly end up behind bars. Also what the role of the social work practitioner is and how they can work to address some of the oppressive and discriminatory factors that impact on the lives of young offenders.

The child welfare and YJ systems appear at first glance as two separate approaches in addressing the needs of young people. This is reinforced somewhat by the way each system has differing aims and objectives that have resonance with specific service user groups and therefore embrace a delineated intervention focus. Social work with its welfare-orientated approach seeks to engage with vulnerable individuals and groups in the welfare system (Thompson, 2005). The YJS, however, is associated with particular interventions that engage convicted offenders seeking to rehabilitate and reduce crime (Liebman, 2007). This bifurcation is reflected organizationally, with the YJS placed under the control and responsibility of the Ministry of Justice while the welfare system resides with local authority social service departments.

Victims and offenders are also seen as two polarized ends of the crime spectrum; one the recipient of a criminal act and the other the perpetrator of the action. Each of these 'roles' has a number of assumptions associated with it; for example, the former where victims are perceived as helpless and with offenders seen as violent and aggressive. However, social workers know that these views often heralded by the popular press are not so clear-cut, with many young people inhabiting the roles of victim and offender in equal measure.

The aim of this chapter therefore is to highlight the need for a broad under-standing of the lives of young people who enter the YJS to allow for a balanced view of young offenders based on up-to-date research and practice wisdom and not the influence and the perceptions of the media.

Welfare and justice

The child welfare system underpinned by the Children Act (1989) and (2004) oper-ates to safeguard and protect the welfare of children. The Children Act (CA) and subsequent policy and procedures place a responsibility on Social Service Departments to focus on children deemed 'in need' or those who require 'protection'. These defini-tions are somewhat contested (O'Hagan, 2006); however, the salient points from the CA 1989 state that the child's welfare is of paramount importance, local authorities where possible must seek to allow children and young people to live with their families and should work in partnership with parents and families to achieve this aim (Children Act 1989). The duties placed upon local authorities include assessments of children in need and subsequent provision of support services for parenting and care. The Children Act (2004) increased significantly the role of partnership working and monitoring of outcomes between agencies and also introduced the five principles of the Every Child Matters (ECM) agenda that identify the outcomes for children and young people: be healthy; stay safe; enjoy and achieve; make a positive contribution; and achieve economic well-being (Children Act 2004).[1]

The YJS has a plethora of underpinning legislation relating to children and young people who commit criminal acts (Crime and Disorder Act 1998; Youth Justice and Criminal Evidence Act 1999; Criminal Justice Act 2003; Anti-Social Behaviour Act 2003; Criminal Justice and Immigration Act 2008).

The overarching aim of the YJS is: 'to work to prevent offending and reoffending by children and young people under the age of 18, and to ensure that custody for them is safe, secure, and addresses the causes of their offending behaviour' (Ministry of Justice, 2011: 1).

Youth Offending Teams (YOTs) were created by the Crime and Disorder Act (1998) to achieve this aim. Every local authority in England and Wales has a multi-disciplinary YOT made up of representatives from the police, probation service, social services, health, education, drugs and alcohol misuse, and housing officers (Ministry of Justice, 2011). The role of the YOT is to identify the needs and problem-atic areas of a young person's life (10–18 years of age) that may underpin their offending behaviour by assessing them with a national assessment tool, the 'Asset'. This assessment instrument highlights specific areas of concern relating to offending behaviour and this enables the YOT practitioners to identify suitable programmes to address these issues with the intention of preventing further offending.

It is widely acknowledged that the CA (1989, 2004) influenced and impacted on the work of the YJS. However, as a social worker in YOTs there are specific pieces of the legislation that you need to be aware of and these are examined in Chapter 2.

Structurally social workers are creations of the statute and therefore a practitioner working in either the welfare or justice system would for the most part have very different legislation underpinning agency policy and therefore their practice. This variation in practice and intervention reflects core elements of policy and procedures; for example, National Standards for the YJS and the Common Assessment Framework for the welfare system, each shaping social work practice with young people in very distinct ways. These frameworks define the standard required for good practice when working with children and young people on either specified court orders in the YJS or when conducting an assessment of a child's welfare needs and subsequent planning to address them. It will not be too surprising to learn that many children and young people would have been subject to both forms of assessment and intervention at some point in their young lives; for example, research conducted for the Youth Justice Board (YJB) on persistent young offenders showed that 38 per cent had been accommodated by a local authority at some point in their lives, compared with 0.5 per cent of the general population (Arnull et al., 2005).

The involvement of young people in the welfare and justice systems concurrently or consecutively are examined further on in this chapter.

Political context

Successive governments regardless of their political persuasion have called for a variety of ways to address crime in the UK. In recent years the Labour Government with its 'tough on crime, tough on the causes of crime' cry usurped the traditional right-wing ground of the Conservative party who had held the monopoly on increasingly punitive approaches to addressing the perennial problem of criminal behaviour, especially that of youth crime. The current Coalition Government, with its financial cuts to social service budgets, has sought to politicize child welfare and YJ further and as a consequence this continues to establish the role of social work as one of the most political of all professions (Goldson, 2005; Mathews and Young, 2003; Jordan, 1998).

This is set against the contextual backdrop of England and Wales having the highest incarceration rates for young people in Europe (Muncie, 2009). This has been linked to numerous factors relating to legislation and policy implementation that reflects a political stance where youth crime is deemed intolerable and must be dealt with severely (Goldson, 2006). This mirrors the inordinate levels of custody for young people aged 12–17 in this country. The latest figures identify an average figure of 2418 young people in this age range either sentenced, awaiting sentence or remanded at any one time. Eight per cent of this figure will be young females (Ministry of Justice, 2011; Parliament UK, 2010).

A major ethical concern for social workers is not only the numbers of youth in custody but more so the disproportionate number of young people in local authority care who come into contact with the YJS (Youth Justice Briefing, 2007). Figures vary depending on source but all present a negative depiction of the numbers of young offenders with a care history. For example, figures from the YJB suggest that 70 per cent of young people involved in the YJS have a care history or involvement from social services (YJB, 2007: 96). In the case of custody, figures vary with open cases to statutory child welfare agencies as a result of neglect and/or other child protection concerns ranging from 30–50 per cent depending on source (Prison Reform Trust, 2007; Goldson, 2006). Therefore as a social work practitioner in a YOT it is very likely that you will be working with children and young people who have all of the difficulties and issues associated with their involvement in the welfare system with the additional concerns of offending behaviour. Your awareness that the welfare system can act as a feeder to the YJS and that the older the young person the potentially more vulnerable this makes them to incarceration needs to be borne in mind and balanced with the notions of punishment and rehabilitation.

Victims and offenders

It is fairly easy to identify who an 'offender' is or what they have done to be labelled as such; however, it is substantially more difficult to do the same with the term 'victim'. The dictionary definition of victim establishes them to be 'a person or thing that suffers harm, death, etc, from another or from some adverse act, circumstance, etc' (World English Dictionary, 2011). Obviously in terms of the YJS we are looking at a legal definition that would appear under the suffering of harm category as defined in law. However, as we shall see, the YJS encompasses a number of young people who are victims in all senses of the word.

There has been an increasing focus on addressing the needs of victims of crime. The current adversarial justice system does little to offer victims involvement in or a voice about the procedures that they are exposed to. However, involving the victim in the judicial process and subsequent court ordered sentence is becoming more commonplace especially in the YJS (Home Office, 2003).

The wholesale introduction of restorative justice (RJ) interventions has been the cornerstone of implementing a substantially more focused victim approach to involve victims in the punishment and rehabilitation of young people. The influence of the victim's perspective is curtailed in relation to sentencing offenders, although 'victim impact statements' can be read out in court and are deemed to at least allow the voice of the victims to be heard. The sentencing framework used by judges to sentence has a number of checks and balances to allow for fairness and mitigation in sentencing offenders for the same or similar offences. Conversely it is the requirement of judicial fairness for the offender that does not allow for the impact of the offence on the victim to affect the sentence given.

Within the YJS numerous forms of RJ interventions are deployed to allow the offender to make amends for their behaviour. These take place across all manner of pre- and post-court disposals including letters of apology, victim awareness sessions and face-to-face meetings with victims through a variety of mediated processes (Home Office, 2003). Referral Orders were introduced in the Youth Justice and Criminal Evidence Act (1999) and seen as an RJ approach to address less serious crime by first time offenders. The order allows the young person to address their offending behaviour in partnership with a panel of local community representatives and a YOT worker and provides the opportunity for the victim to attend a meeting to express to the offender the consequences of their actions. Many YOTs employ a Victim Liaison Officer whose role it is to engage with victims of crime and assist in identifying interventions that may benefit the victim. In relation to the Referral Order panel they would also provide support for the victim when attending the meeting and/or read out a statement from them highlighting their views on the offence (YJB, undated).

Although the engagement of victims is seen as essential to the initial court process (as witnesses to assist in the conviction of the offender), their role in helping to address youth crime through their attendance in meetings with young offenders has also been identified in more recent years (Home Office, 2003). The duality of their role as one of victim of crime and also interventionist is captured through the RJ process as it is seen as empowering for the victim in allowing to meet the offender and have a say about their feelings regarding the impact of the offence. The Referral Order is considered by many proponents as the means to achieve this aim and is considered as the pinnacle of restorative interventions in the YJS while others are concerned that in practice it lacks some of the core elements that make it a restorative process (Stahlkopf, 2009; Crawford and Newburn, 2003).

Persistent concerns for many observers of RJ are the level of victim involvement and that subsequent satisfaction with the process and outcomes can fluctuate according to geographic location, practitioner workload pressures and commitment to involving victims in the process. However, unless your role is one that encompasses the management of the Referral Order process, it is unlikely that you will work with victims of crime. The focus of the YJS does not incorporate the needs of victims to any substantial degree and traditionally the work of its employees has been to focus on offenders. Victim work can be very rewarding and although somewhat slow and sporadic the involvement of victims in the judicial process is becoming more commonplace. As the focus of the YJS changes, it is possible that the role of social worker in the YOT will become more balanced towards addressing the needs of victims equally.

The notion and definition of who is a victim can be a difficult one to reconcile especially if you shift your view slightly to incorporate a broader definition.

Offenders

Overall figures for the year 2009/10 identify that 106 969 young people aged 10–17 were in the YJS and 198 449 offences had been committed; of concern is that at any one time 2418 young people are held in a custodial environment (Ministry of Justice, 2011). These figures reflect a decrease in youth crime by 33 per cent since 2006. Sixty per cent of all offences were committed by young males aged 15–17 years of age. Young men also accounted for 92 per cent of the prison population of whom 84 per cent were from a white background. These statistics highlight the disproportionate number of young males from black minority ethnic (BME) groups within the YJS and the relatively small number of young females involved in the system (Ministry of Justice, 2011).

Many authors warn of relying on statistics collated from official sources and suggest that this does not allow for an analysis of those areas not within the research scope. For example these statistics only relate to 'proven' offences that are convicted offences for which a young person has received a court disposal. They do not incorporate crimes that have not been reported, go undetected or that were not seen as viable to go through the court process. They also do not identify the social and individual characteristics of the young people involved in the YJS and therefore lack an anti-oppressive and anti-discriminatory analysis of factors that many young people are exposed to. However, official statistics are usually underestimates and in general they correlate well with children and young people's own views of their offending behaviour (Edinburgh Study of Youth Transitions and Crime; see Smith et al., 2001; Smith, 2004).

Official statistics do provide us with a picture albeit incomplete and a starting point to engage with some of the issues that affect young offenders. For example a key theme that threads its way through the lives of many of the young people involved in criminal activity is that of poverty. The 'corollaries between child poverty, social and economic inequality, youth crime and criminalisation are undeniable' (Goldson and Muncie, 2008: 222). Poverty has been identified as a defining feature of many social work service users and a perennial social issue that the social work profession has done little to address or change (Cree, 2010; Cunningham and Cunningham, 2008).

Fyson and Yates (2011) suggest that although the predisposing factors are the same for all young people, those with a learning disability/difficulties (LD) have additional social concerns such as being bullied and so could be more exposed to criminal behaviour. This is expounded by statistics relating to young people incarcerated where one in five has some form of learning disability (Bryan et al., 2007). It has also been identified that young people with LD often originate from lower socio-economic backgrounds as do many young offenders.

Young people in the YJS are three times more likely to have mental health needs than their peers who do not (Hagell, 2002; Arnull et al., 2005). Of concern are figures relating to the mental health needs of young people in custody where Lader et al. (2000) identified that eight out of ten met the criteria for more than one formal mental health diagnosis. Contextually, it has been well documented that young people, especially males from BME groups, are overrepresented within the YJS. It has been acknowledged that they receive harsher sentences and this manifests itself with a higher BME prison population (House of Commons Home Affairs Committee, 2007). There are also disproportionate numbers of BME males with mental health and learning disabilities.

The correlation between non-attendance in school and offending behaviour is well documented. The HM Inspectorate of Prisons 2003 survey identified that 83 per cent of boys had been excluded and 41 per cent of boys and girls were aged 14 or younger when they were last in school. The YJB's (2005) study of risk and protective factors found a considerable relationship between risk factors for youth offending and those for educational under-achievement and this was mirrored in the YJB study of persistent young offenders[2] where low educational attachment, attendance and attainment were found across the whole sample, with 45 per cent known to be regular truants (Arnull et al., 2005). The lack of statutory education is seen as one of the largest factors linked to recidivism (Youth Justice Board, 2005). Given the acceptance of the positive role education has in reducing offending and reoffending rates, the Government's lack of commitment in enforcing legislation that ensures local authorities are responsible for the education provision for young offenders in custody settings is of great concern (Children and Young People Now 2011).

All the data highlights that the majority of crime is committed by males, with females accounting for 22 per cent of all disposals (sentences) given within the YJS in 2009/10 (Ministry of Justice, 2011). At the same time media perceptions identify the offending behaviour of young females to be on the increase and therefore the new societal concern. Arnull and Eagle (2009) suggest that offending rates among young females have not increased per se and can be accounted for by changes in the policing of girls and young women that has drawn attention to less serious anti-social behaviour and brought them more into the purview of the YJS. There has been a trend in recent years for girls and young women to be prosecuted for offences that in the past would not have been prosecutable (Steffensmeier et al., 2005). Therefore it is likely that it is the response to female offending that has changed rather than offending rates themselves.

The most disturbing statistic to be added to the plethora of figures is that of the number of child deaths while in custody. Goldson and Coles, (2008) identified that there have been in excess of 30 child deaths in prison often while the young person is of 'looked after' status by a local authority. Issues relating to the 'duty of care' held by the local authority and broader arguments against any type of incarceration for children manifest themselves around this major concern. The child centredness of the YJS must be questioned given the volume of young people incarcerated, the level of care received while in custody and numbers of deaths against the obvious contravening of the United Nations Convention on the Rights of the Child and the Beijing Rules that clearly identify custody as the very last resort.

Many of the issues that impact on young people's lives such as poverty, ethnicity, gender, disability and mental health concerns will be very familiar to social work practitioners; however, why some or a combination of these factors result in criminal activity is not fully understood. Khan (2010) highlights that many of the risk factors associated with mental health problems and offending behaviour correlate and overlap, for example poverty, lack of education, self-esteem and confidence issues. Also official research statistics highlight that many young people who are victims of crime (69 per cent) state that the perpetrator of the offence was another young person under 18 years of age (Philips et al., 2009). Arnull and Eagle (2009) also found that the victims of crime committed by girls were most usually other young people, and often those known to them. In addition the Crime and Justice Survey 2003 identified that young offenders are more likely to become victims themselves (Wood, 2005) and other studies have consistently noted high levels of previous victimization among young offenders (Arnull et al., 2005).

Research has established that no one factor can be specified to cause criminal behaviour (Anderson et al., 2005). However, there are a number of identified social, biological, structural and legal factors including poverty, gender, offending peer group, family (encompassing inadequate supervision), offending family members, lack of education, abuse, loss, foetal alcohol syndrome or other brain trauma, mental health difficulties, and alcohol and substance misuse that are prevalent to varying degrees in the lives of young people who commit criminal acts (Cormack, 1996; Feilzer and Hood, 2004; Smith, 2006; Arnull and Eagle, 2009).

Many of the factors that potentially influence a young person to offend are also the elements that appear to increase the risk of victimization and this appears especially salient in relation to poverty and lack of community resources (Muncie, 2009). Muncie suggests that there is an interconnectedness between these two groups as 'victims and offenders are from the same populations and victimization is related to particularly risky lifestyles' (p. 170). In addition the key attributes that predispose individuals to commit crime are often prevalent to varying degrees in the everyday lives of social work service users (Hornby, 2003). What factors or combination of factors cause one young person who has many or all of the issues outlined to offend, while another not, when both appear to have experienced some or all of the factors above, is a complex issue and not within the remit of this publication (Arnull and Eagle, 2009). Suffice to say, however, that criminological and social work research has established a correlation between these difficulties and issues and a predisposition for some young people to go on to commit anti-social behaviour.

Implications for social work practice

Practising as a social worker in the YJS is different from practising in more traditional social work settings such as child welfare. The age ranges, birth to 18 (and sometimes beyond) for children in the welfare system and 10–18 years in the YJS reflects the structural and socially constructed nature of children, childhood adolescence and youth (Best, 2005). The age range of young people in the YJS will invariably be that of teenagers and adolescents with all the issues that entails and which encompasses age-related and culturally defined societal assumptions, along with physical and psychological milestones of development (Llewellyn et al., 2008).

It is also probable that you will be working predominantly with males and, depending on geography, the ethnicity will be reflected in or overrepresentative of the local populations. This may well be an area that is unfamiliar for many practitioners as the tendency for social work practitioners is to mainly work with younger children or with a different service user group entirely. There is also very little literature regarding social work with this age group.

In terms of your interaction with young offenders it is our contention that as a social worker in the YJS you may need to develop a broader view of who is a 'victim' by moving away from the traditional notion of someone who has experienced crime in the eyes of the law to one that encompasses a broader definition in terms of lifestyle and limited choices. This in no way is to diminish the devastating effects of crime or their impact on victims but many of the young people with whom you will work in the YJS will be both victims and offenders and thus it is important that you understand this context and approach young people in this way. Doing so offers a more nuanced and complete way of defining the service user group that you will be working with.

You will also need to be aware of the role of personal and structural oppression and discrimination that has affected the lives of many young people who offend. Child deaths in custody, the lack of educational provision, the disproportionate number of young males from BME groups in the YJS and the numerous individual and structural characteristics explored above highlight areas of major ethical and values concerns for social work practitioners. Given the value base and ethical nature of social work practice these concerns will resonate with the traditional aims of social work empowerment regarding particular marginalized groups and individuals.

Summary

As you can see, there are very good reasons why Youth Offending Teams (YOT) are required to employ a social worker. A theoretical understanding of crime and offending behaviour does not assist in changing young people's circumstances, attitudes and life chances, and research into the lives of young people who commit crime highlighted a number of significant areas that require professional social work intervention.

Although essentially the same responsibilities are assumed in both the welfare and justice settings, the work and interventions associated with the differing systems means that the daily engagement of a social worker with children, young people and their families in the YJS is very different from that of a social work practitioner in the child welfare system. Your role in the YOT is to address both the welfare needs and the offending behaviour of the young person and it can be a difficult task to balance your obligations to the service user, employer and broader society.

Social workers or associated professions involved in the YJS also need to reflect on their own personal and professional ethics and value base when working with young offenders (this is explored in more depth in Chapter 3). The broad overarching intentions of social work and other helping professions to empower, engage with and act in a non-judgemental manner, while promoting the well-being and interests of young people within an anti-oppressive and anti-discriminatory framework can be lost or diluted amid the constraints of a punitive system of accountability and responsibility.

Notes

1 For a more comprehensive description of the Children Act(s) please refer to Johns (2007) and Brayne and Carr (2008).
2 This term now usually referred to as 'frequent'.

2
Legislation

```
LEARNING OUTCOMES

By the end of this chapter you should be able to:

•    Appreciate the complexity of legislation and its impact on practice.

•    Examine how ethical social work practice can be achieved within statutory frame-
     works.

•    Utilize Thompson's PCS approach to highlight Anti-Oppressive Practice (AOP)
     and Anti-Discriminatory Practice (ADP).
```

Introduction

The Crime and Disorder Act (1998) initially underpinned the current youth justice system (YJS); however, there have been numerous additional pieces of legislation and policy that either supported the 1998 Act or were subsequently implemented after its introduction and impact on the work of Youth Offending Teams (YOTs) and its practitioners.

The aim of this chapter is not to examine the historical evolution of youth justice (YJ) and child welfare legislation; this has been comprehensively undertaken elsewhere (see Dugmore et al., 2007; Goldson and Muncie, 2008). Neither is it to explain nor delve into each piece of legislation listed in Table 2.1 to examine the myriad of connotations that this may yield for YOT practitioners. The aim of this chapter is to identify and demonstrate the multitude and complexity of the wide-ranging statutes that create the systems (welfare and justice), and dictate the role and services that YOT workers provide and the policies and practices that prescribe interaction with young people. The previous chapter outlined many of the substantive characteristics of victim and offenders; this chapter explores the construction of these demographics employing Thompson's (2006) personal, cultural and structural (PCS) Anti-Oppressive Practice approach and how this can be utilized in practice.

The chronological history of the evolution of legislation and the perpetual arguments surrounding the taxonomy of 'welfare' and/or 'justice' or 'need' versus 'risk' are the consistent themes that permeate through most publications relating to YJ (Crawford and Newburn, 2003; Pickford and Dugmore, 2012). This is especially pertinent for social work that ultimately is not a 'do nothing' profession, whether dictated by legislation or by the desire to act ethically and in the best interests of marginalized and vulnerable client groups, social workers' raison d'être is to intervene to alleviate suffering and hardship.

The rationale that legislation and subsequent policy guides and aids our actions in a particular circumstance is a simple and effective premise; however, when faced with two sets of contradictory legislation and guidance surrounding the same social group, in this case children and youth, how are actions to be decided? From a social work perspective this is somewhat mitigated (or complicated) by the professional codes of ethics, values and practice that can assist workers when faced with potential practice tensions in their daily work lives (GSCC, 2008; BASW, 2012). It is understandable that the considerable array of standards, codes, ethics, and legal and welfare frameworks can feel overwhelming and intimidating for social work and YOT practitioners.

Table 2.1 sets out numerous pieces of legislation, reports and guidance that require consideration when working with children and young people who are involved in either the child welfare system or YJS or potentially both.

Table 2.1 Youth justice and child welfare legislation, reports and guidance

* Misspent Youth: Young People and Crime (Audit Commission, 1996)
* No More Excuses: A New Approach to Tackling Youth Crime in England and Wales (White Paper, 1997)
* Crime and Disorder Act (1998)
* Statutory Instrument 2000 No. 1160 (introduced the YJB's planning, commissioning and placing function)
* Youth Justice – the Statutory Principal Aim of Preventing Offending by Children and Young People (1998) – arising from the Crime and Disorder Act
* Misspent Youth '98: The Challenge for Youth Justice (Audit Commission, 1998)
* Misspent Youth '99: The Challenge for Youth Justice (Audit Commission, 1999)
* Youth Justice and Criminal Evidence Act (1999)
* Criminal Justice Act (2003)
* Anti-Social Behaviour Act (2003)
* Every Child Matters and Youth Justice: The Next Steps (2003)
* Children Act (1989, 2004)
* Youth Offending: The Delivery of Community and Custodial Sentences (National Audit Office, 2004)
* Youth Justice 2004: A Review of the Reformed Youth Justice System (Audit Commission, 2004)
* Youth Green Paper: Youth Matters (2005)
* The Criminal Justice and Immigration Act (2008)
* Positive for Youth (2012)

Other relevant legislation that impacts on the work of YOT practitioners are the National Assistance Act (1948), the Housing Act, (1996), the Data Protection Act (1998), Children (Leaving Care) Act (2000) and the Homelessness Act (2002).

Legislation can somewhat address the need for clear and firm boundaries when engaging with young people; however, social work practitioners also need a critical appreciation of the broader media-generated public perceptions of youth and young offenders. Predominantly, these negative views of adolescence and young people are obviously not reflective of all youth and historically have principally focused on male working-class lower socio-economic young people. It is this social group and its association with poverty and marginalization that will particularly resonate for social workers across all spheres of social work practice.

YJ social work

Social workers on completion of their training should have a comprehensive understanding of the law in relation to child welfare legislation especially the Children Acts (1989 and 2004) along with the evolution of the Every Child Matters (ECM) agenda, as they all place children at the centre of social work practice. Once qualified, a social work practitioner wanting to work in the field of YJ would have to embrace another raft of legislation. Workers may have had a placement in a YOT and therefore have some idea of the work involved but many workers engage in YJ practice with an initially limited comprehension of the role. As you can see from Table 2.1 there are multiple Acts and policies that surround the role of YJ practitioner and nothing highlights more the ethical dilemmas of being a social work practitioner in the YJS than the complexity of the legislative frameworks that surround and guide the practices within it. The social worker needs to be competently aware of the differences in statutes and cognizant of the interplay, overlap and contradictions that can play out in YJ practice. These frameworks are at best conflicting, establishing value-laden views of children and young people who are perceived to be either in 'need' or at 'risk'. It is also the arena where social work principles and values are at most risk of being compromised, dissolved or diluted (Dugmore et al., 2007).

From a structural perspective the plethora of legislation allows reflective practitioners the opportunity to assess how social workers and associated practices, service users and the system they inhabit, are all socially constructed through the statutes. This formation of statutory roles and responsibilities defines the parameters of social work practice, creating service users and subsequent and associated interventions (Cavadino and Dignan, 2005; Johns, 2007). This ultimately results in the creation of the deserving and undeserving (or eligible and ineligible) categories of service users who are produced through the processes of assessment and specific eligibility criteria. Therefore transgression of social norms through the breaking of society's laws and the ensuing interventions identified through the YJS and National Standards to address that behaviour ultimately dictate responses that determine the processes of crime and punishment. A distinction is clearly fashioned (despite the rhetoric) through the welfare and justice discourses that young people in trouble are not the same as troubled young people. The contradictory message that YJ provision is considered a part of children services while also separating the practices of welfare and justice is a persistent and incongruous one.

As macro (structural) processes subsequently impact on micro level (personal) interactions, it is essential for social workers to be aware of the implications that legislation and policy have on specific service user groups. The formation of policy and legislation may not always address the issues it was intended for and often there are unforeseen consequences to its implementation (Arnull, 2012a). However, the systematic discrimination of specific societal groups, especially those who are poorer and from ethnic minority groups, highlights shortcomings in the current approach to addressing youth crime (Goldson and Muncie, 2008).

Practitioners require an awareness that the legal parameters set by law and which define what is and what is not considered a criminal act are not always equitable for all members of society. This resonates with 'labelling' theory that examines how the transgressing of agreed and acceptable societal norms creates deviancy and in turn assigns meaning to that behaviour. From this perspective, deviancy is seen not as the quality of the act committed but as how that act is viewed by others (Becker, 1963). For example, once individuals are given a label, for instance that of criminal, victim or perpetrator, then they are viewed as such by society. This negates them and marginalizes their ability to function as fully integrated societal members. Legitimate activities such as school or employment may be denied them, forcing them to perpetuate their label (Becker, 1963). This sociological crime theory expounds the view that the justice system along with society creates more criminals than it deters (e.g. Anti-Social Behaviour Orders (ASBOs) seen later in this chapter).

There are some deviant acts that are not viewed as serious as others; for example, white-collar crime, considered to be the domain of corporate business and the rich, encompasses the crimes of tax evasion and insider trading which have been seen as difficult to police due to their monitoring by other parts of the state structural apparatus, such as commissions and are often regulated by civil not criminal law (Sutherland, 1962; Stenson, 1991). This structural discrimination highlights where the emphasis is placed on criminal behaviour and reflects a multi-tiered justice system that focuses mainly on the crimes of the poor while those of the rich including corporate crime go relatively unpoliced (Eitzen and Maxine, 1986). Although there have been some efforts by regulating authorities to pursue corporations through the criminal law system it is clear that 'the preoccupation of the criminal justice systems of the advanced societies [is] with low status offenders, the moves against white collar crime and corporate crime remain sporadic and uncystallized' (Cullen et al., 1987: 353). In addition, given the nature of these offences it would be rare for young people to even have access to the resources to commit these crimes and this further reinforces where the gaze of the crime prevention services rests.

As stated in Chapter 1, social work often does little to address the socio-economic factors that contribute to many of the predisposing issues that are potentially explanatory factors for young people's involvement in committing crime especially poverty, ethnic groupings and class (Cree, 2010; Cunningham and Cunningham, 2008). It continues, despite its mandate, to work with individual service users addressing perceived psychopathological traits in their character that cause them to act in a deviant manner requiring treatment and rehabilitation. It is therefore remiss in attending to the wide-ranging factors that impact the service across a spectrum of structural components.

This is reflected by the considerable criticism directed at the justice and welfare systems, the former because of the potential to discriminate and draw particular societal groups into its purview, especially in terms of race, culture and gender (see Chapter 1). The latter has been criticized for the freedom given to professionals working with young people who with very little substantiated evidence can enforce major life-changing decisions on children under the heading of 'best interests' of the child. Therefore disempowerment, the disenfranchising and the marginalization of youth occurs within each system and requires the practitioner to have a greater under-standing of the legislation surrounding welfare and justice and how it can potentially impact either individually or collectively on young people.

One example of this is the ASBO that historically is linked to the 'broken windows' theory, which was first developed by two American academics, Wilson and Kelling (1982). These academics stated that there was an obvious link between disorder and crime and in neighbourhoods where there are visible signs of decay – litter, broken windows, graffiti and abandoned housing – this signals public disinterest. This resulted, they argued, in a fear of crime being greater in these areas and with the detri-mental effect of prompting 'respectable' community members to leave. The theory demands that even minor misdemeanours must be pursued with the same vigour as serious crimes and this ultimately gave rise to the 'zero tolerance' approach to addressing youth crime. This was reflected in Tony Blair's 2005 election rhetoric when he said that 'I want to send a very clear signal from Parliament, not just the govern-ment, that this type of disrespect and yobbish behaviour will not be tolerated any more'. He later introduced the Respect Action Plan that was launched a year later and built on the drive to tackle ASB and reclaim communities for the law-abiding majority.

Much has been written about ASBOs and for the most part a practitioner in a YOT will not be involved in an application for one of these orders imposed on a young person. However, they will need to be aware that the conditions stipulated within the order may have far-reaching and oppressive consequences on many service users (Goldson and Muncie, 2008).

What constitutes ASB has been a contentious issue since the orders were introduced with very broad definitions allowing for much youth (and adult) activity to be interpreted negatively and punished quite severely. Broadly, ASB is acting in a way that causes or is likely to cause alarm or distress to one or more people. To be ASB, the behaviour must be persistent. Examples include: rowdy, noisy behaviour, 'yobbish' behaviour, vandalism, graffiti and fly-posting, dealing or buying drugs on the street, fly-tipping rubbish, aggressive begging, street drinking and setting off fire-works late at night (Directgov, 2012). ASBOs can be imposed pre- or post-conviction and can have a wide range of conditions attached to address the ASB. These can include exclusions to certain geographic areas, congregating in groups or associating with specific individuals. To complicate matters further there are numerous agencies that can seek an ASBO application; for example, local authorities, police forces and registered social landlords and housing action trusts.

ASBOs have been criticized for blurring the boundaries between civil and crim-inal law as many orders that were granted were initially civil in nature with the breach of conditions becoming a criminal concern (Dugmore et al., 2007). Although the intention of the ASBO is to reduce ASB, the conditions and requirements imposed can on occasion have a counterproductive effect. If the young person's YOT or school is in the exclusion zone identified, or if the young person needs to get on a bus to school with other youths identified as part of a non-contact requirement, then the order becomes unworkable and ineffective. The oppressive and discriminatory nature of ASBOs was promptly realized and despite the overall rate of youth crime falling, the breach rate of ASBOs reached 70 per cent and would often result in 'a trapdoor' to prison, increasing youth custody rates rising to a point where the system almost collapsed (Guardian, 2012).

After a groundswell of criticism that the ASBO impinged on young people's human rights as many of the conditions imposed were draconian and the punishment of non-compliance with those conditions exceptionally punitive, their use began to diminish in 2005 with applications steadily falling ever since. The current Coalition Government's approach to addressing ASB appears to follow Labour's Respect Agenda somewhat although the use of ASBOs is no longer as prominent; it has recently launched the 'Troubled Families' programme that also seeks to address such issues as crime and ASB, worklessness, education and health. Local authorities will receive up to £4000 for every family they work with successfully under this payment by results programme. The intention is that this money will finance the early transformation of services to the benefit of the programme and identified families (Fineberg, 2012). Practitioners will want to be aware that the implementation of these types of programme as with ASBOs may have far-reaching and as yet unforeseen outcomes.

A useful tool to identify discriminatory and oppressive policies and practice such as the ASBO and its effects is Thompson's (2006) PCS model that views oppressive practices as occurring on three levels: personal, cultural and societal. As Table 2.2 identifies, the personal level (P) encompasses interpersonal relationships, personal feelings, attitudes and self-conceptions, and interactions between individuals, which as seen from the table correlates with practice relationships (Payne, 2005). The personal is intrinsically linked to the cultural context (C) where norms and rules that establish how the person feels about themselves and others along with interactions between people and the environment are played out. The personal and cultural levels are then fundamentally embedded within the societal framework (S), which forms the structures, norms, rules and order within society.

As illustrated below the structural elements define the systems of work and while acknowledging that social work cannot in itself change these structures, it can highlight how these arrangements impact services users on the other two levels and

Table 2.2 Thompson's (2006) PCS model

P: Personal	C: Cultural	S: Structural
Psychological	Commonalities	Social division
Practice	Consensus	Social forces
Prejudice	Conformity	'Sewn in'
	Comic	Socio-political

therefore contribute to good reflective practice. This model can be applied quite easily to given practice situations and policy issues across both systems and can be used as the lens to view interventions that are potentially oppressive.

For example, one area that the welfare and YJ systems uneasily coexist is that of Secure Remand. This is a bail option where a young person is remanded into secure accommodation (a custodial facility) and as they are not convicted of any offence are considered 'looked after' children by the local authority. This means that at this point in the judicial process the local authority has the responsibility for the well-being of the young person that encompasses a duty of care along with the financial costs of their incarceration. Once the young person is convicted, the responsibility shifts to the Youth Justice Board (YJB) and although a social worker may still be involved with the young person, the duty of care is transferred to the YJB secure environment. These scenarios are not frequent but can cause some consternation as the process of getting a young person remanded into local authority Secure Remand is a protracted one, with decisions often taken at a very senior management level due to the financial implications for the local social service department. Even before the current financial cuts to social service budgets, many local authorities would not have welcomed the additional costs that this type of bail option incurs. These situations highlight philosophical, practice and financial divisions between these two children's services and do little to enhance partnership and collaborative working as emphasized by the ECM Green Paper and the Children Act (2004).

A structural example of the dominance of the Criminal Justice System (CJS) relates to the overarching aim of the Children Act (2004), which was to co-ordinate all the relevant children's services in one geographic location and this required the remodelling of services into the creation of new local structures such as 'Children's Trusts' and Local Safeguarding Children Board (LSCB). The LSCB has the main responsibilities as set out in section 14 of the Children Act 2004 to co-ordinate and quality assure the safeguarding children activities of member agencies and monitor whether 'local partners, through the Children's Trust Board, are effectively safeguarding and promoting the welfare of children and young people in their local area' (Munro, 2011: 53).

It was acknowledged that YOTs would be a crucial component of the Trust and LSCB if services for children were to be integrated; however, surprisingly, they were not initially included in the pilot study. It was argued that YOTs needed to be separate from other children's services if they were to maintain their success and therefore over time it became apparent that YOTs would not be fully integrated into mainstream children's services. In seeking to assuage this divide, it was reiterated that YOTs would work more closely with the spectrum of children's services thus improving accessibility to services for young offenders and enabling YOTs to contribute to the broader aims of the social inclusion agenda (YJB, 2004). This reflects that although change was sought at the structural level to enable all services to work in concert with each other, the politicization of crime and welfare continued to differentiate how services were viewed and deployed.

This bifurcation in service provision reflects the ongoing debate identifying whether youth offending matters and/or welfare concerns could or should be addressed within specific welfare or justice frameworks, each with their conflicting ideologies (Farrington, 1984; Goldson, 2005). Research shows that there are a multitude of potential factors that contribute to youth offending emphasizing the welfare aspect, while accountability for one's own actions and the safety of the public stresses the need for judicial interventions. These two strands of welfare and justice are viewed very differently in the literature and in practice (Harris and Webb, 1987; King and Piper, 1995; Pickford, 2000; Crawford and Newburn, 2002).

As stated previously, these statutory processes create frameworks for practitioners and assessments. At times they overlap and at other times they conflict and appear incompatible; regardless, they establish guidance and a set of criteria for distributing services. What is not often captured are questions surrounding those families or young people who do not fit the frames/criteria for aid, such as refugees and asylum seekers who may have been refused entry to the country and therefore have no recourse to public funds. This may manifest in individuals lying about their age, stating that they are younger than they actually are to avoid possibly harsher adult sentences or to enable them to access welfare services such as counselling that they require due to their circumstances and are more readily available in the YJS. When presented with circumstances where people cannot legitimately gain access to services or finances, it is not difficult to understand why individuals seek illegitimate means (crime) or lie to survive. Consequently, despite the best intentions of some policies and legislation such as the Children Act (2004) and ECM, some children or youths will inevitably fall through the safety net and one of the unforeseen consequences of these and other policies is that this can lead to subcultures and what has often been derogatorily referred to as the 'underclass' where criminality and ASB are the norm (Muncie, 2009).

On a positive note, one of the successes of the YOT is its multidisciplinary approach to addressing youth crime. The Crime and Disorder Act (1998) dictated the criteria for specific professional groups to define the YOT. These groups were often supplemented by other professionals from an array of statutory and voluntary backgrounds such as youth work and arts practitioners. However, with the introduction of the Children's Trusts and the reduction in YOT budgets this may mean that YOTs will reduce the staff team to core personnel and therefore diminish the intervention options available to young people to address their offending behaviour. If YOT capacity diminishes this will impact local authority social service departments as YOTs will have to make more referrals into mainstream services and therefore place a considerable strain on ever decreasing resources.

At a time of major financial cuts, the increased need to do more with less may not correlate with the desired legislative goal of partnership and collaborative work that underpins the ECM and Positive for Youth agendas.

Summary and critique

It is hoped that the content and albeit brief excursion into legislative frameworks will allow an opportunity for the reader to reflect on how social work and its respective service user groups are created through the statutory mechanisms of assessment and eligibility criteria. In addition, despite the intention of legislation to combine child welfare and youth justice services under the new 'Children's Trust' and Local Safeguarding Children Board structures, financial considerations along with long-standing established incompatible professional boundary issues may undermine its effectiveness.

A thoughtful critical consideration of what is and is not seen as deviant behaviour and which groups are more prone to being drawn into the focus of both child welfare and YJ systems would also aid the practitioner in their social work career. The additional caveat is for workers to be mindful of those individuals and groups who for whatever reasons do not (even when they meet the criteria) come to the attention of statutory social services because of their citizen status or who dishonestly try to obtain services as the lawful process of access is not available to them. These scenarios can be usefully examined with Thompson's PCS model as it illustrates that ADP and AOP take place across a number of domains and not just on the personal level, where social workers are most likely to intervene, but may also take place on the cultural and societal levels as these levels are embedded within each other. Social workers often working at an individual level are able to challenge discrimination and oppression, but may find it more difficult to change discriminatory and oppressive behaviours of larger groups of people, such as a group with a shared culture or society as a whole that continues to discriminate and oppress. Social workers can begin this process by first examining and reflecting on their personal views, culture and societal norms, rules and structures.

The Fasbo exercise below highlights the paternalistic nature of both welfare and justice approaches with major assumptions made about the ability of some individuals or couples to parent. It also reflects that some of the roles that social workers inhabit may not correlate with the values and ethics of the profession. As Dominelli (2002) points out, social work can be viewed contradictorily as an oppressive caring profession. Therefore utilizing Thompson's PCS model YJ and the child welfare systems along with the role of the social worker can be examined in relation to AOP and ADP.

EXERCISES

1   Read the article: 'The nursery rhyme police – parents to take lessons in reading and singing' which is available online at www.thisislondon.co.uk/news/article-23374380-the-nursery-rhyme-police—parents-to-take-lessons-in-reading-and-singing.do
     Divide into groups of two and discuss whether you feel that the idea of 'Fasbos' and the use of 'Parenting Orders' is beneficial to parents. Consider the capacity for particular families to meet the conditions of the Order and also consider the socio-economic impact of fines and eviction on those families if they are unable to comply. Will this Order be used for all families?
     Class to regroup and discuss their answers.
2   Using the generic case study on page x, apply Thompson's PCS model using the three categories of oppression to identify which, if any, areas apply. Can the PCS model also be used to view the Fasbo article and what does it tell you?

3

A multidisciplinary approach

LEARNING OUTCOMES

By the end of this chapter you should be able to:

*   Appreciate the complexity of multi-agency practice.
*   Examine how social work judgements are informed by ethics and reflection.
*   Understand the role of research in informing social work practice.

Values and ethics: the challenges of care and control

This chapter highlights how social work manifests itself in the youth justice system (YJS) and introduces partnership and multidisciplinary work within the YJS. The intention in establishing Youth Offending Teams (YOTs) (Crime and Disorder Act 1998) was to bring together the different professionals working with young offenders into one team to encourage and facilitate effective inter-professional practice; it was also anticipated that young people would gain from the professionals' increased understanding of one another's roles and there would be less duplication of work. It was also an attempt to mirror the complexity of need that many young offenders demonstrated and provide a holistic response.

The role of the social worker within this multidisciplinary approach is therefore predicated on the notion that social work values are intrinsically something that practitioners would bring as a professional group to the YJS, and thus that the social worker will within their professional role: show Respect, Empathy and a Commitment to Social Justice; facilitate as appropriate, Self Determination and Empowerment; ensure their practice is Non-discriminatory and Non-judgemental, based on Reflection, Theory and Evidence (BASW, 2012).

As we have seen, youth justice (YJ) work underwent a sea change in 1998 under the Crime and Disorder Act 1998 (CDA) that made multi-professional approaches to working with young offenders compulsory because of what was perceived to be the multidimensional aspect of youth offending (Chapters 1 and 4). Additionally, the ability to work effectively with other professionals became a key feature of generic social work practice throughout the late 1990s and early 2000s, with inter-professional practice enshrined in policy and legislation across the social policy spectrum, including for example children and families work as directed by Every Child Matters (ECM) (HM Government, 2004).

The reason that a social worker would have had cause for intervention with a young person through the YJS was that the young person had transgressed and broken the law. The new feature post-1998 was however to also 'prevent' offending (Liddle, 2008). Research presented by agencies and professional groups working with young offenders suggested that a significant proportion of young people in the YJS were also young people 'in need' (Children Act 1989) and/or who had experienced significant structural disadvantage, such as poverty, race, poor education, health or lack of opportunity, and so on (Farrington, 1996). The implication of this was that there were ways of identifying those at 'risk' of offending and intervening with them at an early enough point to be 'prevent' them offending. The multi-professional approach sought to ensure this by bringing together professionals with skills in dealing with crime, social need, health and education. The intention was to overcome the structural separation that existed between these services and achieve a 'joined-up' approach (HM Government, 1999).

Some, such as Dugmore et al. (2007), argue that within the YJS there is an 'irresolvable' tension between welfare and justice approaches that is specific to YJ work and which by implication makes it harder to apply social work values. We would argue this is not the case for there is a tension, which lies at the heart of all social work practice. That tension is most palpable where social workers exercise care and control functions: balancing the concern for the individual alongside a concern to uphold state values regarding 'acceptable' behaviour. These tensions might manifest, for example, with regard to the levels of care that are considered acceptable for a parent to give to a child, or a carer to an elderly or disabled person, or with regard to establishing someone's mental health and fitness to make decisions for themselves or live within the community. On each occasion the social worker is asked to form a 'judgement'. There is therefore an intrinsic tension in the very notion of social work.

Social work frames its values to allow social workers to form these 'judgements' while also upholding the rights and freedoms of others: often working and intervening with those who have less power and are less able to uphold those rights for themselves for structural reasons (BASW, 2012). The agreed acceptance in the professional role of the social worker is of the right to form a 'judgement' and to 'step in' when occasion demands on behalf of the state/society while ensuring the human rights and dignity of the individual are maintained. However it is framed, this is the legitimization of the social worker's role.[1] As we saw in Chapter 2 society agrees a set of codes, laws and statutes and through these creates a role for social workers whose role is then to ensure those basic standards of care and levels of access to social provision (e.g. Children Act 1989). Within the YJS social workers are asked to work with those who have infringed society's laws (e.g. Crime and Disorder Act 1998): the social work role is therefore to consider how the young person can be 'punished' while also upholding their rights and advancing their empowerment in order to allow them to be rehabilitated and function more effectively in society (see discussion in Chapter 4).

The voice of the service user

The tensions described above lie at the heart of social work and demonstrate the importance for social workers to be clear about their role and themselves. A strong core understanding enables them to effectively reflect on what the state is asking them to do and to know if they consider that reasonable. Challenges and questions are important and can come in many forms; for example, radical social work, research, radical and service user movements such as feminist, psychiatric system survivors and disability rights campaigns (Beresford, 2010: 228) and other campaign groups large and small, for example Barnardos. The importance of service user and campaign groups is that they help to challenge the day-to-day assumptions of social work practice. They offer a balance, an external reflection, enabling practitioners to continually ask themselves: 'in doing this do I continue to uphold and advance social work values?' In this, social workers in the YJS are again no different from other social workers; in some ways because the tension in their role is so large it is easier for them to keep this tension to the fore.

There are many significant campaign groups concerned with the wider criminal justice system in the UK, namely Nacro and the Howard League, among many others. The former has campaigned a lot on YJ and, as we shall explore below, had a significant impact on the formation and shape of the current Youth Justice Board (YJB) and system through documents such as Wasted Lives (Liddle, 2008). However, despite the recent rhetoric around customer and service users, which has been common post-Thatcher in social policy (Beresford, 2010), there has been little specific service user consultation/input into the YJS other than as research participants. However, recently the YJB, Children's Commissioner and User Voice (2011) funded 'User Voice' to do some work to seek the views of young people in the YJS. Their rationale in so doing was that:

> Young people have an ability to speak extremely openly and honestly. They are unafraid to challenge the status quo and offer the insights that we require to commission services that best meet their needs. If we fail to seek the views of children and young people in custody, then we fail in our duty as commissioner of their secure estate.
>
> (YJB, Children's Commissioner and User Voice 2011: 3)

Seeking young people's views in this way is a new approach for the YJB and it will be interesting to see how it advances. It challenges the notion of an entirely carceral state body, doing 'to' users, in seeking service users' views on criminal justice penalties; however, it may also irritate some who would consider it offends the notions of 'punishment'. In itself therefore it neatly illustrates the tensions in the YJS – between care and control; nevertheless, the end aim is to increase effectiveness and increase compliance, which it might be argued is in the state's interest as well as the young person's.

Ethics, reflection and research in the YJS

Within the UK there are a number of ethical codes that provide a framework for social work practice. Currently the Health and Care Professions Council (HCPC) provides the overarching remit for practice,[2] and professional bodies such as the BASW lay down the ethical codes. The British Association of Social Work (BASW) is an umbrella body and its ethical code is modelled on and reflects that of the International Federation of Social Workers. The BASW has recently reviewed and updated its ethical code (2012); this contains a notion of challenge, a watchful awareness, reflexive practice in which the practitioner consistently examines what they are asked to do in society's name and to balance this and compare it with their code of ethics; those practising within the YJS are no different.

The current way in which the YJS is organized is, as we have seen, the result of significant campaigning by left leaning and socially aware charitable and third sector organizations in the 1990s with the changes enshrined in the CDA 1998. Since then there have been specific changes, for example, to the sentencing structure. In general the overall design has remained much the same, especially assessment, in the form of Asset, which underpins the whole structure on which young people are progressed through the system (see Chapter 4). Although there have been academic (Arnull, 2012b; Muncie, 2009) and practitioner criticisms and critiques of current forms of work and assessment within the YJS, there have been few major[3] practitioner challenges. Writers such as Arnull et al. (2007; also Baker, 2005) argue that the potential power that Asset brings has not been garnered or used as effectively as it could have been. Their research showed that data collected through assessment could be used to effect policy and practice change and lead to strategic responses. They highlighted how those working within the YJS could use information at their disposal to identify need and feed into wider social policy planning mechanisms:

> The aggregation of the three Asset domains of Living Arrangements, Family and Personal Relationships and Neighbourhood can usefully identify the individuals and the population of young people who are in housing need or at risk of having housing problems.
>
> (Arnull et al. 2007: Summary: recommendations)

There has also been considerable criticism of working practices within social services, the YJS and the Criminal Justice System (CJS), which are often portrayed as increasingly managerial and depoliticized systems (Muncie, 2009; Feeley and Simon 1996, Davies, 2002). This is most often characterized as new public management (NPM) or McDonaldization; such terms seek to describe what they characterize as lower levels of professional discretion, increased bureaucracy and management intervention, often linked to computerized record-keeping practices, such as the Integrated Children's System (ICS). Others, such as Giddens (2001), argue that New Labour's modernizing approach to government has been more concerned with regulation than domination and writers such as Arnull (2007) and Glendinning et al. (2002) claim that there is evidence of multi-agency partnerships and organizations finding sophisticated ways of using the information available to them to plan and influence provision that meets

local need and addresses inequality. Their findings suggest that it is possible for creative practitioners to find 'spaces' in which to challenge bureaucracy and ensure they
are supporting and empowering service users; finding solutions to problems by
exploiting funding streams for their own planned uses through creative approaches.

Information collected through forms of assessment, such as Asset, can be used to
provide clear evidence of structural hardship (e.g. housing) and the data is available
to practitioners and easily collated. That it has not been used by social workers more
effectively to date to influence provision, strategy and as a campaign tool, may say
more about the way social work has been practised. Many social workers come into
practice because of their interest in people. They want to help individuals and focus on
them; however, were they to make use of data at their disposal it would be entirely
consistent with their ethical codes and remit for practice. The challenge it seems is for
social work to more enthusiastically embrace a learning and research culture as it is
currently urged to do by the Social Work Reform Board (SWRB) (2010) and Munroe
(2011). Should this approach be inculcated into social work practice it would empower
social workers to use the information in their systems and utilize this information to
effect policy change and campaign for service provision.[4] Where there are excellent
examples of practice that is creative, social work needs to highlight and celebrate these
as effectively as possible.

Developing research skills can only be of benefit to social workers and does not
have to be time-consuming and can greatly enhance practice. The new framework of
capabilities for social workers emphasizes areas of knowledge, critical reflection and
analysis, professionalism and ethics and the ability of the social worker to be an independent, critical thinker, aware of current research and able to account for the judgements they form in a professional way (Professional Capabilities Framework (PCF)
narrative 2012). The lessons from research can moreover be straightforward and easy
to implement. For example, research undertaken in 2005 for the YJB said that some
young people had negative experiences with their social workers; these experiences
were characterized by the young people as a lack of consistency and contact, illustrated by social workers not telling young people they were leaving a post and would
no longer be the young person's social worker; when the young person next made
contact or arrived at the social work office they would find their social worker gone
(Arnull et al., 2005). This was clearly bad practice, but it was common enough for
young people to generate this issue without prompt. The experience caused significant
distress to young people, many of whom had histories of loss and broken relationships
and so steps to address it formed a recommendation in the report and summary.

However, in 2011, Munroe undertook interviews with young people for her
report on the state of social work in the twenty-first century; unfortunately, she found
young people telling of similar experiences. Munroe (2011) suggested that young
people were distressed by this experience and her findings showed that the
recommendations made by Arnull et al. (2005) were not heeded and this aspect of
'practice' was not 'put right'. The findings of Arnull et al. (2005) and Munroe (2011)
are not the result of managerial practices in social work and it can be too simplistic for
managerial cultures to be held solely to blame for poor practice. In both pieces of
research the key factors leading to poor practice were a lack of reflection and effective
communication with service users that led to a failure to uphold values.

Some have argued that in order to improve practice we need an 'emphasis on the ethic of care' (Barnes, 2011: 15) and this is a recognition of social work values. Managerialism, pressure of work and a 'prevailing emphasis on the ever-increasing and time-consuming demand for accountability through computer and paper recording' (Barnes, 2011: 15) may well be blamed on occasions for poor practice. But as social workers our values urge us to give respect to the service user and to challenge unfair or discriminatory practice – it may be that we have all at times done the job at hand and not asked the question, if I was empowering and enabling what would I do now? But if we did, the answer might simply be that we would more effectively use the information we had to hand to campaign for better housing provision or make a few straightforward calls and send letters to young people when we were leaving. As a practitioner in the YJS, in a system that can be experienced as powerful and oppressive, it is important for social work practitioners to be able to find the spaces to challenge discrimination and structural inequality and use the information they have to empower.

Reflection and youth justice practice

This reflects a dilemma for the social work practitioner whose focus may move during the course of any intervention from that of advocate for the young person to that of adviser and enforcer to the courts. However, this is an oversimplification, for the social work role is that of the social worker in court and thus the intention is to bring to the role their professional values and ethics. The social worker should be the person who advocates for the young person within the court and judicial system ensuring that the sentence is one that addresses the underlying causes of offending and is commensurate with the offence. The social worker's remit in this is therefore different from that of colleagues from other professions and disciplines. The nature of social work is to be an empowering process and that is complex and arguably more so within a judicial system where an aim is also to punish transgression. Nonetheless, it is clearly the social worker's role to access appropriate services, ensure Anti-Oppressive (AO) and Anti-Discriminatory (AD) practice and offer challenges to decision- and policy-makers to ensure a fair and just YJS. Maintaining this social work focus within a punitive system is not always easy for practitioners and that is why a clear sense of professional duty and ethics is important. Reflective practice is obviously a key element in this and should form an ongoing and cyclical element of practice (see Figure 3.1).

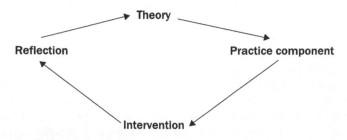

Figure 3.1 Reflective practice diagram

Theorizing about reflective practice derived originally from education but has become a popular concept in social work practice in recent years; nonetheless, there are many social workers who will have trained before it was common. Donald Schon (1983) is the theorist who devised the concepts of:

1   reflection-in-action;
2   reflection-on-action.

We should act consciously, thinking about what we are doing, as we do it (e.g. in assessment and intervention) – '*in action*' and should also think about and reflect on the assessment or intervention once we have done it – '*on action*' in order to be able to be clear about the reason for assessment/intervention and then to consider what was effective, what less so and what might be done differently. Others have built subsequently on the work of Schon, and this includes Thompson and Thompson (2008), who suggested a third element:

3   reflection-for-action.

Thus that we should plan in advance ensuring that theory and practice are brought together and be able to demonstrate 'how theory underpins practice and practice informs theory . . .' (2008: 21). These notions are also those shown to be key elements in effective practice.

The intention is that the practitioner should be open to a more critical view of themselves, theory, their organization and practice and so challenge practice based on 'assumptions'. The social worker should engage in conscious and explicit practice that is demonstrable and for which they are accountable. The suggestion is (drawing on Thompson and Thompson, 2008) that the practitioner is aware of both their 'practical competence' and their 'professional artistry'.

Theorists in reflective practice consider the practitioner as responsible for their own learning and practice: Moffat (1996: 50) argues that 'If the social work student investigates practice reflexively he or she can experience a sense of agency even within the most constraining environment'.

Clearly this is important in a system that we have suggested can be oppressive or restraining. A social worker within the fast-paced and often politicized atmosphere of YJ needs to ensure that they continue to practise in a way that leads to 'open knowledge'. Thompson and Thompson (2008) have termed this 'open-mindedness' and suggest it has three elements:

1   The explicit use of knowledge which is able to be scrutinized and challenged.
2   Is not based on fixed ideas.
3   Incorporates a willingness to learn from strengths and weaknesses.

Authors on reflective practice argue that 'critical reflection' incorporates a sense of questioning and places practice in its wider socio-political context. 'Critical' is therefore intended in its analytical sense. Proponents of reflective practice say it is:

- transformative;
- emancipatory;
- allows for the construction of new narratives.

Moffat (1996: 53) argues that reflective practice is important because:

> students are taught the logic of the detached professional and they bring this logic to their practice. There is the risk that the social work student will impose his/her knowledge as a type of master narrative which subjugates the story of the client and undervalues the knowledge from which the client draws to understand his or her circumstances.

Clearly such practice would not be empowering or support the anti-oppressive value base of social work. Additionally, Taylor (1996) defines reflective learning as something that enables us to explore our '. . . experiences in order to lead to new understandings and appreciations'. She suggests that this can be 'creative and intuitive' leading us to become 'confident in responding to the unpredictable and unknown'. Such a skill base would be important to a social worker facing the many different challenges that working in the YJS can pose.

The roles of the social work practitioner

Social workers play a number of different roles within the YJS and these include:

- report writer;
- court officer;
- supervising officer.

These roles are underpinned by the social worker's professional training, values and ethics as we have discussed above. The individual aspects of each role are addressed in the relevant chapters; for example, assessment, interventions and court, but the underpinning skills will be explored here. The social worker brings their generic social work skills, drawing in particular on key foundations such as communication and listening. Their role within the YJS is to enable the young person to explore in a safe and conducive atmosphere the issues and actions that have led the young person to the place they currently are; that is, the meeting with the YJ practitioner. The practitioner must draw on their knowledge of all forms of communication, including verbal, non-verbal, para-verbal and empathic and active listening (Beart et al., 2011: 19). This means that whether the meeting that is taking place is in order to write a report, plan or undertake an intervention, it is imperative that the practitioner thinks about and responds to what the young person says, the way they behave and the manner in which they express themself, showing interest and conveying concern. In order to do this the practitioner must be on time, prepared, aware of background circumstances and information, have undertaken and ensured any specialist support/access is available, have given due time and consideration to the meeting and follow-up work and ensured that their questions/intervention is relevant, focused and the purpose understood by the service user and others who may be accompanying or supporting them. The practitioner must be prepared to tell the young person how they see things; for example, what realistically the outcomes might be or what the implications are for them as a result of the behaviour that has led them to this interview/intervention (Lishman, 2009: from Beart et al., 2011). In so doing the practitioner conveys and demonstrates their listening and communication skills, and ensures that any barriers to effective communication have been considered and planned for. They also demonstrate their social work values, reflective and AO and AD practice.

Within the YJS the social worker is called upon to demonstrate their skills in communicating with young people, as well as other professionals and families. As we have seen elsewhere in this book, many of the young people we meet in the YJS have had experiences of victimization, loss and structural inequality; they may have been accommodated by the local authority or had numerous experiences of social services or other outside health and welfare agencies, as well as having learned ineffective or anti-social coping mechanisms. They might find it easier to express anger than other emotions and may have other needs, including learning disabilities. All of these present challenges when seeking to interview the young person for a focused intervention like a court report or to work with them to plan an intervention that they may not welcome or regard as warranted. Underpinning social work values and communication skills are therefore essential, enabling the worker to 'get alongside' (Richards et al., 2005) the young person, or to enable them to understand the options they have, as well as the restrictions that will apply (Freire, 1972). This is directly applicable and practitioners within the YJS should ensure they are confident in doing this and able to communicate with young people and families who are distressed, agitated and angry. There are a number of techniques and methods that can be used by practitioners, and social workers in the YJS should ensure they have these skills and are appropriately trained. There are too many to discuss here, but a number of the techniques are based around acronyms and ones such as SARAH devised by Lambert (1996: from Beart et al., 2011: 29) are especially pertinent, suggesting that the interviewer Stops talking, Actively listens, Reflects content and feeling, Acts with empathy and Handles objections by listening to those, reasoning and dealing with the objections.

Other professionals within the YJS: multidisciplinary working

Underpinning all of the above is a concern to ensure effective, reflective, AO and AD practice that is client centred. Social workers will work alongside team members and colleagues who are police officers, youth workers, health professionals, teachers and specialists in identified areas (e.g. mental health, substance use, educational psychologists). The social worker, as we have seen above, brings core values, ethics and skills that underpin their work. It is essential that they are clear about these as this will facilitate their effective engagement with others, enabling them to understand what colleagues from different professional backgrounds bring, to value the differences and be able to offer challenges where they consider these are appropriate.

In so doing the social worker will communicate more effectively with their colleagues thereby facilitating multidisciplinary and inter-professional practice. As we have seen within a generic social policy framework, the ability to do this effectively is now a requirement, but for the social work practitioner within the YJS it will be core business.

Multidisciplinary and multi-agency practice within the YJS is recognition of the need for a holistic approach to young people who offend and who have multiple needs. The specialist advice and support that each team has can vary tremendously. Additionally, some areas now have YJ practitioners who have undertaken a youth justice qualification that is below graduate level but which aims to give some training to those working within the YJS in what might previously have been unqualified positions (they are often entry points for later social work qualification training). Because each YOT is a product of its local services and 'owned' by those services it is their decision who forms the YOT and this leads to considerable local variety within a core of posts. 'Managers (primarily) need to work with local partners to raise awareness and demonstrate need' (Mason and Prior, 2008: 50) in order for the YOT to be as effectively staffed and integrated into local services as possible. Understanding this, we can also see how important it is that staff within the YJS understand research methods, effective practice findings and how to use the data at their disposal, in order to be able to argue persuasively for resources; the better they are at doing this the more effective their partnership will be (Arnull, 2008).

The roles that other professionals play within a YOT may be very similar to that undertaken by the social worker, or may differ and be quite separate – this is usually decided locally. However, roles ascribed to each professional are usually:

- Police officers – are most likely to be involved with young people at the reprimand and final warning stages and at times may supervise Referral Orders. They will also be responsible for obtaining previous convictions.

- Probation officers – will usually work with 16–18-year-olds and undertake similar duties to social workers: assessments, Pre-Sentence Reports, supervision.

- Youth workers – were expected to be a feature of YOTs but many no longer have them and this in part reflects the fact that many youth services have been drastically cut. However, it is also the result of a professional view that some youth services have taken; withdrawing from statutory services/involvement (YOTs) in recognition of the voluntary nature of their engagement with young people and which underpins their professional ethos. Where the youth service is involved it is often with the Youth Inclusion and Support Programme (YISP), where youth workers may run the drop-in service or staff the facilities. Social workers might also refer young people to youth services outside of the YOT.

- Health professionals – were anticipated to play a major role but this too has varied: in some areas they provide specialist treatment, for example substance use, mental health treatment, or provide a referral route to other specialist support such as educational psychologists or for assessment for speech and language assessment or learning needs. Because health assessments should also be undertaken where appropriate they may also play a more generic role.

- Specialists in identified areas may come from specialist services or the voluntary sector – for example, mental health and substance use – or this may be provided as above. Often the team will have a formal link with the Child Adolescent Mental Health Service (CAMHS) but this may not mean a specialist worker attends the YOT – again this varies considerably by area.

- Education, training and employment (ETE) advisers – these were provided by Connexions who were designated workers. Some areas retained Connexions, but not all and thus once again specialist ETE support will usually be provided but in different forms. Mason and Prior (2008) highlighted how difficult it is for young offenders to get access to high-quality ETE support and thus how essential the effectiveness of multidisciplinary working and relationships are to obtaining this for young people supervised by the YOT.

- Housing – finally, some areas do have dedicated housing support and advice either within the team or as a nominated person. However, some areas, for example, may decide they do not have a housing need among young people and may not provide any nominated link. Again the effectiveness of the YOT in demonstrating need and lobbying for resources is important.

The variation in provision for YOTs with regard to multidisciplinary teams is a reflection of local need, the effectiveness of strategic relationships at a senior level and local political priorities. It is essential for senior managers to set an expectation of close joint working for this to be effective and then for local managers and staff teams to agree with partners:

- roles, responsibilities and expectations;
- protocols and service-level agreements (SLAs);
- how information and data will be shared, including confidentiality, routes for communication, procedures for sharing information and referring cases.

The agreements and arrangements should be formalized as and where necessary. Research indicates that where there is a history of effective joint working this is most likely to percolate down and across all sectors (Arnull, 2008).

Additionally, the system of case management has come to the fore across the social and health care systems, in part in response to multidisciplinary approaches to work. The YJB's own 2008 guidance into effective case management states that: 'Case management is similar to casework, but builds upon that approach to include partnership and multi-agency working, and the co-ordination of a programme of support as an integral aspect' (Mason and Prior, 2008: 5).

Mason and Prior further suggest that in order to achieve holistic support for young people '. . . youth justice practitioners are likely to need to refer to other agencies and organisations to ensure that their inter-related needs are met' (2008: 33), and that case management facilitates ongoing work allowing the practitioner to look for other options and vary the interventions undertaken and so facilitate effective engagement because, for example, their progress or achievements are noted and rewarded – perhaps by being able to take part in a new activity (2008: 44).

EXERCISES

Using the case study example (p. x) imagine you have made a home visit at 3.30 p.m. when J (the girl) has arrived home from school and her mother had said she would be available. On arrival you find the mother drunk. The mother says during the interview that people are making a fuss over a few bottles of soft drink that she could easily pay for and that she thought the shopkeeper was simply reporting her daughter because she (the mother) had fallen out with him some months previously. The mother says they are unpopular locally because the area is 'posh' and people think they are 'not good enough' because the father is black and she, the mother, white. The daughter looks very uncomfortable during your whole visit and tries to deflect her mother from raising these issues – she is told to shush and looks nervous and constrained. During the visit the mother becomes more agitated and eventually abusive to you as an 'interfering do-gooder'. She says that they 'don't need you poking about in their business'. At this point you end the interview, saying it really is time you were going, but that it might be necessary to contact them again in the future; you tell the young person you will be in contact to see her again, but this time you will need to meet with her at the office.

When you return to the office you are a little shaken and concerned that you could have done something differently or prepared more for the interview, but there had been nothing to indicate the mother would be drunk, angry or abusive. You have supervision tomorrow and want to take this case and decide how best to take forward the matters raised by the meeting. Before you do that you decide there are a number of steps you need to go through to prepare.

Imagine yourself doing this now, and on your own or as part of a group complete the following reflective techniques:

- Draw a detailed mind-map – consider each person and part of the scenario – what factors may be at play?

- 'Imagine' the situation differently: write an account from the perspective of the mother, daughter, father and shopkeeper.

- As far as you can recall write down what you said just prior to and during the parts of the interview where the mother became increasingly agitated. Think about all the forms of communication – verbal, non-verbal and para-verbal, empathic and active listening – was there anything that could have communicated to you the mother was becoming more agitated or why? What other non-verbal or para-verbal cues or active listening skills might you have used at this point?

- Finally, think about the possible barriers to effective communication in this scenario; for example, physical, psychological, cultural, language or environmental factors that influenced the meeting? What were they? How might you prepare for those?

Notes

1   This is why it is so important for social workers as a profession and as individuals to be quite sure about their values and be able to form 'judgements' about the acceptability of what they are being asked to do on behalf of the state. It is also why there is an inherent

tension between social workers and the state – negotiating for example levels of provision, risk and care to children or in the case of adoption balancing long-term outcomes and identity, both current concerns in the UK with the Coalition Government.

2   The GSCC will change and become the HCPC in 2012 but its remit is not yet defined.

3   It is acknowledged that there may be many day-to-day challenges and questions, and some have been brought to our attention in the writing of this book, but these are rarely visible on a national scale.

4   This approach is taken for example in the medical and nursing professions.

4

Risk

LEARNING OUTCOMES

By the end of this chapter you should be able to:

- Appreciate the complexity of risk and protective factor research.
- Understand how risk and protective factor research has informed the YJS and how it can be examined through the lens of AO and AD practice.
- Be able to reflect upon the welfare and justice, care and control debates and form an argument about this.

The focus in this chapter is on risk: to the young person and to society in general. The interventions, which it is said will reduce those risks, are explored in more depth in the two following chapters. Picking up from the previous chapter, this chapter also reflects the debate on the broad issues of welfare and justice, care and control. We explore how risk is defined and focus on risk factors and the research that defined them and underpinned the assessment framework, Asset, which is at the core of all social work assessments in the YJS. We also consider whether through a social work professional lens, especially within an Anti-Discriminatory Practice (ADP) and AOP framework, the definitions of risk correlate with that of the YJS.

Defining risk

The Youth Justice Board (YJB) (2005) funded work that drew together the research on risk and protective factors which had been identified in numerous pieces of research and which were said to be associated with offending. In part they did this because research on the functioning of the YJS suggested that practitioners, whose work was underpinned by that research, did not appreciate or understand how it linked to their forms of assessment and interventions (Arnull et al., 2005; Baker,

2005). The idea therefore was to bring together what was known and make it available to and intelligible to YJ practitioners.

Risk is seen to be located within four domains:

1   Family
2   Community
3   School
4   Personal or individual factors.

Examples of the risk factors included within these domains are:

- Family – large family size, low levels of parental supervision and high levels of conflict between parents and a child.
- School – low levels of achievement, poor attendance and high levels of aggression/ bullying.
- Community – disadvantaged neighbourhoods, low income levels, high levels of overcrowding, high turnover and low levels of local attachment.
- Young person – hyperactivity, impulsivity, low levels of cognition, alienation, lack of pro-social attitudes, attachment to delinquent or anti-social friendship groups (YJB, 2005).

Factors can also be described as static, that is, unchanging, or dynamic, i.e. changing. You will later see how each of these elements has influenced the development and construction of Asset.

As we discussed in Chapter 3 much of the work that has been undertaken on risk factors has included longitudinal, prospective or retrospective studies and these continue to influence current work in this area. Prospective studies have found it harder to definitively use the identified factors to predict behaviour and often result in a high proportion of false positives (see further discussion below). However, the retrospective studies show a high correlation between identified risk factors and the characteristics of the sampled populations. Put simply, those who are offenders will have the characteristics that comprise identified risk factors; the difficulty is, so will a considerable number of other people who do not go on to become offenders. Work now also emanates from the USA and Australia where risk-based work has received attention; it is important to bear in mind when reading such studies that the social, welfare and criminal justice systems (CJSs) are different and thus one should pay attention to the details included.

Farrington (2000) researched the identification and use of risk factors alongside a methodology that sought to assess them and to intervene. He argued that his ideas could be used to identify factors relevant to individuals and their offending and to ensure that the appropriate people were targeted for specific interventions. This has since received considerable academic criticism (e.g. Haines and Case, 2008) and this is discussed in more detail in Chapter 5. As noted above, although risk factors may denote a likelihood of later offending, most of those who also have those same char-acteristics will never offend. The calculations of risk are based on probability and the evidence is emergent; much has been done on risk but the tools are being consistently refined and improved; for example, how can we understand better whether particular risk factors in combination will lead to certain outcomes? At this time risk factors are better at identifying risks across a group than identifying particular individuals and thus when using the tools it is essential to remember this. The young person may have characteristics that for a group of individuals indicate that their probability of behaving in a certain way in the future is elevated; but this does not mean that this particular young person will. Because it is not yet possible to predict or identify the salient factors adequately, much interest has focused in recent years on resilience. Thus, why when dreadful things happen or a high conglomeration of risk factors occur in someone's life do they appear to live happy, non-offending, settled lives when the research would suggest the probability of such an outcome is low? Risk factors can only indicate that someone may commit offences in the future – they cannot tell us that this will happen. It is important for social workers to recall what they know about research generally and be aware both of false positives, suggesting that it is almost certain that a young person will become an offender, or false negatives, suggesting the risk is low (Munroe, 2011). It should also be acknowledged that actuarial assessments are important tools and the predictive accuracy for Asset with regard to recidivism is about 60–70 per cent (YJB, 2008: 17). It is therefore reasonably accurate – but it does not tell the whole story; however, it is an indicator among others, including profes-sional judgement.

In terms of the social worker's role, this is the time for their training to become apparent and be utilized to help them and other colleagues to use the tools (such as Asset). It is the time for the skills discussed in Chapter 3 to come to the fore and your 'practical competence' and 'professional artistry' (Thompson and Thompson, 2008) to be displayed. Alongside social work values, which give agency to an individual and suggest that with the right support, life may be what they want to make of it.

Protective factors

As well as risk factors, there are also protective factors (another term for resilience, though not always used as such). It is argued that these reduce the risk of offending because they lower the likelihood of other risk factors, lessening their negative effects. Factors such as self-esteem and self-efficacy are seen to be important along with an access to other/new opportunities (Rutter, 1987). Clearly, these are highly congruent with social work aims and welfare-based approaches. Their acceptance within the Youth Justice Board (YJB) and the YJS accounts for their inclusion in Asset and is why those factors are also 'counted', but in academic circles and internationally they remain the subject of significant discussion and debate. For example, how might risk and protective factors interact with one another? What about risk and protective factors that we have no influence over, such as gender? How can programmes support protective factors and reduce risk? For example, does placing a girl on her own in an offending behaviour group with boys undo the protective factor of gender and elevate the risk factors (Arnull and Eagle, 2009)?

However, an acceptance of protective factors are to an extent the premise on which social policy programmes such as Every Child Matters (ECM) (2004) are based, that each child should:

- Be healthy
- Stay safe
- Enjoy and achieve
- Make a positive contribution
- Achieve economic well-being

Large prospective studies such as the Edinburgh Study (Smith and McAra, 2004: 3) show this to be appropriate. The intention behind ECM (2004) was that each professional working within the social care sector (including the police) should act to ensure the five outcomes, thereby reducing risk to children and young people and increasing protective factors. It took a holistic view of the lives of children and young people and sought to ensure that agencies and professionals worked together towards common aims; in this it mirrored the developments that had taken place in the YJS since 1998. Again it can be seen that this is congruent with and influenced in particular by social work theories such as systems and ecological models (Brofenbrenner, 1979).

New Labour who were responsible for the YJB (1998) and current YJS and for ECM (2004) can be seen to have accepted the risk-based work and allowed this to influence their social policy direction (Arnull, 2012b; Garside, 2009). It is congruent with their Fabian, socialist basis that seeks to mitigate and counter structural discrimination, embracing conceptions of agency and looking for long-term, welfare-based solutions. It also supported their concerns for social cohesion post-Thatcher, their notions of a modernized state (HM Government, 1999) and their conceptions of a need to reinvigorate 'respect' for the self and others (Arnull, 2007, 2012b). It was argued that risk-based research could provide empirical data that said that factors could be identified and thus tackled. Those who proposed this believed that in so doing we could 'prevent' harm. They argued that some things were 'done to' some children and young people and some they were responsible for, and that if you were able to identify both and affect their relationship to offending behaviour, then you might be able to intervene and change the future trajectory of the young person. This work influenced the social policies that New Labour built and which form the current structure of youth justice (YJ) work.

Risk: assessment and Asset

The adoption of a risk-based framework of assessment was influenced by a radical agenda that embraced risk-based academic research (Farrington, 1996, 2001; Burnett and Roberts, 2004). It was in keeping with the Effective Practice agenda that dominated criminal justice in the 1990s and early twenty-first century, but it differed from them. Fullwood and Powell (2004) argued that the difference between the probation and prison service approach and the approach of the YJB was that the latter sought to ensure an effective multi-modal method of working whereas the prison and probation service focused on the development and use of accredited offending behaviour programmes. Those programmes (similar to risk-based research) were heavily influenced by psychological conceptions of behaviour and change.

It might also be argued that for the YJB the focus on assessment and a risk-based approach was derived from their emphasis on the prevention of offending; within this scenario assessing the risk of future offending could be seen to be particularly important. Prior to the creation of the YJB and the Youth Offending Teams (YOTs) (1998) the voluntary and campaigning sector brought together and funded research that argued that it was important to work more effectively with young people who were offending, on the premise that many were also young people 'in need' who required (or already received) a number of interventions from state agencies. Additionally, work by the Audit Commission (1996) said that interventions were ineffective and that young people in the YJS had multiple needs. Allied with this the research by Farrington[1] (1996) was based on the premise that young people 'at risk' of offending could be identified by a range of 'factors' that were both structural and incorporated individual agency.

It was argued that by identifying young people showing risk factors it might be possible to intervene early and thereby prevent them from offending or further offending. This notion was the underpinning rationale for crime prevention and appeared to be generated by welfarist concerns. Ballucci (2008) suggests however that risk-based actuarial tools 'unintentionally' result in surveillance. Nonetheless, the focus on early intervention (across the social care spectrum of work with children and young people) has remained and forms part of the rhetoric of the Social Justice Strategy announced in 2012. It is also important to recall that the creation of the YJB was widely hailed by the YJ voluntary and campaigning fraternity as were the underpinning crime prevention imperatives. Thus a report undertaken by Nacro and the Prince's Trust in 1998 argued that: 'Early intervention would mean fewer crimes, fewer victims and less work for the courts and prisons', and that 'A great deal of youth crime had its roots in severe family and educational problems' (Liddle, 1998).

Youth crime could be seen to be derived from multiple forms of deprivation and risk-based assessment was a way to 'capture' that range of data. Baker (2005) showed that when completing Asset there were few variations across professional groups and it would be expected that over time, as multidisciplinary working became ingrained, this would be strengthened. Asset was established as a reliable assessment tool although evidence about practitioners revisiting and updating their assessments has consistently suggested this is a weaker area of practice (see Chapter 5).

Further research by Baker (2007) challenged the notion that the completion of Asset led to routinization of practice. She suggested that in fact it relied on the use of 'clinical judgement' (p. 81) with: 'practitioners asked to make decisions about a wide range of issues . . . gathered in a way that engages a young person and their parents/carers, thus challenging staff to work in a creative and dynamic way'.

How effectively or consistently this work is undertaken by practitioners in the YJS is discussed in the following chapter on Assessments.

Risk: welfare or justice?

It has been argued that there are tensions deep within the foundations of youth justice policy because the young person is seen to have 'agency' – the ability to decide for and act for themselves – and at the same time structural analyses are applied – that the young person/behaviour is impacted by the result of structural factors such as poverty, race, class, gender and ability. There are suggestions that concepts of 'agency' are allied with justice approaches and 'structural' explanations with welfare ones, and thus that there are flaws within the YJS, which is not following one path. However, this is too simple a dichotomy and the YJS as currently constructed is more complex than that: both agency and structural explanations form the core elements that make up Asset and seek to guide the practitioner in 'weighing' these relative factors: this leads to a combination of both justice and welfare approaches (see Chapters 1 and 2). Giddens (1984) argues that this is generically true within the CJS where welfare and justice explanations have historically struggled for ascendancy and this tension can be seen to have applied to responses to young people and offending since the nineteenth century (Littlechild and Smith, 2008).

What is also clear is that it is not obvious that either approach offers the 'correct' or only solution; Littlechild and Smith say that social work and welfare approaches were in the ascendant in the 1970s and 1980s and appeared to lead to poor outcomes and 'net widening' that had a particularly negative effect. The problem when this occurred appeared to be that young people were 'treated' for structural deficits such as poverty and racism and in so doing the effect appeared to be to reinforce rather than ameliorate them: for example, through stigmatization of having been drawn into the YJS in the first place making it harder to get education and work in the future. Arnull and Eagle (2009) wrote of their concern that this was happening in response to girls who committed violent offences in England and Wales but who appeared to have few welfare needs. Net widening has been a concern in the USA too but there the concern has been that girls are drawn into the system as the result of welfare needs, thus for 'running away'. The tensions between welfare and justice approaches therefore go to the heart of many justice systems. Given that most young people in the YJS are victims as well as offenders (Chapter 1) arguably both justice and welfare approaches should be present.

More recently 'strengths-based' approaches seek to affect the relative weight given to justice and welfare explanations, enabling the service user's strengths to be supported and facilitated thereby increasing agency and enabling the amelioration of structural factors. The reasoning for doing this is that it is argued the tendency has been to assess 'deficits' and not strengths and they would criticize both welfare and justice approaches in this regard. Current discussions about assessment in the YJS look as though they are influenced by this approach and seek to build on it (Teli, 2011).

The Children's Society press release for March 2012, in response to the Riots Communities and Victims Panel report, highlights the issues raised by young people's offending: namely whose fault is it? Is it theirs – for it is their behaviour that has brought them to this point? Or is it society's – for failing them?

It is of little surprise that this independent report has pointed to factors like lack of opportunities for young people as causes behind last summer's riots.

The Children's Society's own research has revealed that many young people believe that poverty and disadvantage were one of the key reasons behind the August riots. We know from our work that there is a significant link between a child's material deprivation and their overall life satisfaction.

(The Children's Society, 2012)

As we have seen the YJS and many commentators in the area debate and seek to balance the two perspectives: welfare or justice?

Delinquency and anti-social behaviour (ASB)

Discussions that underpin theoretical criminological explanations of offending talk more traditionally of delinquency and in the British sense delinquency has meant 'naughtiness' or transgression – not necessarily criminality.[2] If as a practitioner working with young offenders you begin from a notion of delinquency as a common, transitional, developmental phase between childhood to adulthood (Mason and Prior, 2008) it can be a helpful way to balance, reflect upon and consider the behaviour at hand. Remember in this phase young people are experimenting with boundaries, responsibility and self-expression.[3] The Edinburgh Study (Smith et al., 2001) found that for many young people aged 12–13 delinquency was not uncommon, that boys' and girls' behaviour was more similar in this regard (than when younger or when adults) and that it was closely linked with other transgressive or delinquent behaviours such as smoking and drinking. There was also a strong association with victimization (see Chapter 1) and poor relationships with parents, in particular low levels of supervision and high levels of conflict. This suggests therefore that delinquent behaviour should not be immediately dismissed by social work practitioners within the YJS, but should be properly assessed and underlying causal factors considered.

Another important consideration when working and reflecting on young people, the tools you are using and society's current concerns, is that notions of delinquency vary over time, as do acceptable behaviours. Burney (2006) has explored the differential response to certain behaviours over time and place, and has used spitting as an example; bear in mind too that a child knocking on someone's door and running away was until recently considered silliness, not ASB.

ASB has become a huge concern in recent years, appears to have crossed political boundaries and was the terminology used by the Coalition Government to account for the riots of 2011. And yet much of the behaviour in the riots was criminal and this serves to illustrate the confusion that has arisen. However, Roberts (2006) highlights how criminal behaviour and ASB are different. Nonetheless, it is important to remember that many young people within the YJS may be subject to simultaneous penalties or interventions; for example, in 2012 the Coalition launched the 'Troubled Families' Initiative that targets multiple levels of deprivation and dispossession through a systemic, multi-agency and community-based approach.

ASB is a descriptor of behaviour that became a focus of policy under New Labour (1997–2010) and arose from concerns about social functioning and society and has been linked with concepts of community. ASB was seen to be located in particular within certain communities (usually poor) and was seen as a signifier of or precursor to criminality as and arising from structural as well as personal or family deficits (Parr, 2011). In this ASB has many links to New Labour's approach to crime and youth offending: Parenting Orders and family-based interventions are for example common interventions in response to both types of transgression. Some have portrayed the responses to ASB as harsh and carceral drawing on Foucauldian concepts while others have pointed to the very real benefits that have accrued to families from the interventions. Parr's (2011: 728) exploration of this with regard to recipients of a Family Support Service nicely illustrates the tension between the care and control functions exercised by the staff and how this was experienced:

> while it cannot be denied that the project entailed the surveillance and supervision of vulnerable and marginalised families in their domestic private spaces, the project also appeared to contain a significant welfare ethos based on finding long-term sustainable solutions to individuals problems . . .

Parr describes the tension for the social (or care) worker in ascribing relative weight to agency and structural explanations. Social work values recognize this tension and urge us to use the knowledge and evidence we have to counteract and campaign for policies which reduce structural inequality (BASW, 2012). Social work practitioners in YJ have at their fingertips a system, Asset, which because it measures need, risk and structural factors can be used to support social work values and form the basis of policy campaigns.

Risk, AO and AD practice

It is important that you think about where you consider culpability lies before you engage in work in this area. Social work's own ethical and values base would suggest that some weight at least is given to the structural disadvantage that many young offenders will have experienced; but our values also urge us to acknowledge the agency that service users have and to seek to empower them to draw on and develop this to help them counter disadvantage. Offending can and does cause real harm and it is important that those working within the YJS help young people to think about, understand and accept responsibility for their behaviour, helping them to form strategies for living effectively in the community without causing harm to others.

Multi-Agency Public Protection Arrangements (MAPPA): assessing high-risk offenders

Managing young offenders who have been assessed as posing a high level of risk is now an inter-professional area of practice bringing a number of practitioners together.

Asset and actuarial tools have less predictive accuracy for high-risk offenders because they measure high-frequency events more accurately than low-frequency ones. High-risk offenders and prolific offenders are reasonably uncommon and therefore the tools that can predict their future behaviour are less accurate, but where the risk posed by the person's potential ability to commit another serious offence or high volume of offences in a short time is considerable, the practitioner is tasked with ensuring that the risk of potential harm is mitigated. In such cases structured clinical assessment has been shown to be most effective; this both draws on social work skills and highlights their importance within the YJS. The YJB argues that within the current system such assessments are conducted using '. . . frameworks which are empirically based and informed by research . . .' (YJB, 2008: 19) and that Onset, Asset and OASys allow for this to occur, with clinical judgement then informing the decision/recommendation made.

Additionally, the YOT practitioner and/or manager will liaise with other professionals to ensure that the risk of harm is minimized by drawing on the knowledge, skills and resources of other social and health care professionals and those within the justice system. This may be informal, but may also include a formal route known as MAPPA (Multi-Agency Public Protection Arrangements). This forum allows the YOT to manage the highest-risk young people with the support of other professional colleagues and is anecdotally seen as important in supporting YOTs with young people whose risk they could not otherwise manage.

YJB (2008: 18) says that as a result of MAPPA there has been 'an increased responsibility on youth justice workers to ensure that assessments are comprehensive and well-evidenced', and although they suggest there is evidence that the predictive accuracy of current tools is increasing, they recognize that professional assessment skills remain the most valuable tool to date.

MAPPA is composed of representatives from probation, police, prison (known as the responsible authority) to assess and manage the risk posed by sexual and violent offenders. Other agencies who would normally be involved are the YOT, education, housing, social services, health and NHS Trusts, social registered landlords and home detention curfew/electronic monitoring providers. The principles that govern MAPPA are to:

- identify who may pose a risk of serious harm;
- share relevant information about them;
- assess the nature and extent of that risk;
- find ways to manage that risk effectively, protecting victims and reducing further harm.

There is a MAPPA co-ordinator in each area and they are the individuals whose job it is to receive referrals and decide if a case meets the serious harm and imminence criteria. If it does they will organize a meeting that they will then chair. The criteria cover three categories of offenders:

1   Registerable sexual offenders, regardless of the sentence they received (Category 1).
2   People convicted of a violent or other sexual offence (even if nobody was actually hurt), who are not registerable sexual offenders, with a 12 month or more prison sentence or hospital order, for a Schedule 15 offence (Category 2).

3   Offenders who do not fall into either of the above categories, but are considered by the authorities to pose an ongoing risk of serious harm to the public based on their past behaviour (Category 3).

The offender will know that they are subject to MAPPA (although not necessarily that they are discussed or considered at MAPPA) but a family is not routinely told and will only be told if the MAPPA meeting authorizes disclosure; they make this decision on the basis of what they judge to be in the best interests of the family. The exception is if the person has been convicted of murder when they must inform any future partners or employers of this. Each person subject to MAPPA has an offender manager, who is based in the probation service (once released from custody) and an offender supervisor based in the prison probation department while they are in custody.

EXERCISES

1   Look at Asset and identify three risk factors that weigh structural deficits and three based on 'agency'.
2   Think about the case study on page x– list the risk and protective factors you could identify for the young person.

Notes

1   Interestingly, Farrington's academic background was also in psychology and thus it might be argued that this is why he, and others influencing work with offenders at this time in the adult CJS, took a more individual approach to tackling offending than a sociological explanation of crime might suggest. However, under New Labour approaches such as Sure Start did seek to tackle structural, social factors and provide an interesting counterpoint to what was happening in the CJS.
2   That is more commonly meant in American usage
3   Clearly, serious crimes, such as murder and assault, do not fit into this category.

5
Assessment

This chapter focuses on the assessment framework used by the Youth Offending Team (YOT) practitioners and how this can at times prove fundamentally challenging for social workers and colleagues who have been used to children- and family-focused assessments. The Asset in its various forms and structure, along with Pre-Sentence Reports (PSRs) and other assessment tools such as Onset, are introduced. As we have in other chapters, we will consider social work values and ethics and think about how ethical assessment and decision-making can be undertaken and achieved in terms of professional and reflective practice.

In this chapter we look at:

- What is an assessment?
- Assessment in the youth justice system (YJS): Asset
- What do people say about different forms of assessment?
- Social work values, assessment and social policy.

What is an assessment?

Assessment is:

- the gathering of information for a purpose, and/or the purposeful gathering of information;
- the analysis of the information gathered;
- the forming of a judgement.

This will usually lead to a written report or recommendation (in a court setting assessments may be verbal: see Chapter 8). It can be something that is a single assessment for a particular purpose; for example, a report for court, an assessment for access to a form of treatment for mental health needs, substance use or housing needs. An assessment may take place over a period of time and include a number of meetings, and it may also involve contacts with other professionals and the gathering of a range of data/information from a number of sources (see Chapter 3). Assessments may be short- or long-term and usually have a defined start and finishing period (e.g. for a court report). However, some assessments may have a number of stages, more commonly where an assessment for treatment is taking place, and they may also be revisited and reflected upon over time by the practitioner and in conjunction with the service user and others; for example, this might apply where interventions are planned and the impact or effectiveness of those interventions is being considered. This may happen when a young person is being considered for release from custody where they are indefinitely detained.

You can see from this that social work practice within the Youth Justice System (YJS) will, as in any other social work arena, encompass a range of forms of assessment and/or involve liaison with other professionals who may undertake other forms of assessment.

The YJB (2008: 8 and 9) describes the risk, need and responsivity framework (RNR) as central to its assessment and intervention strategies (Chapter 4) and these clearly draw on psychological theories (e.g. Andrews et al., 2006). Critics would suggest this also limits these methods – applying individualizing theories and strategizing to universal or structural problems, for example, poverty. The RNR strategy posits that:

1   The **Risk principle** refers to those assessed at higher risk of recidivism; those at lower risk of recidivism require less intensive interventions.
2   The **Need principle** is focused on finding interventions that best meet the needs or problems most closely associated with criminal behaviour.
3   The **Responsivity principle** seeks to match the characteristics of offenders with the interventions they are offered, which may vary from demographic factors to personality 'types'.

As you might imagine, the 'need' principle might on occasions cause concern to social workers who might identify clear 'needs' that are not linked to offending. It is possible to do this within the Asset framework and as a social worker your own ethical and value base should lead you to seek to address these needs once identified. However, the justification that the social worker has for intervening is the offending behaviour and thus it might be argued this should justly be the focus. Changes that are currently being considered for the assessment process are looking at strategies for more effectively signposting young people into mainstream services where other underlying needs are identified. It remains to be seen whether this approach is adopted and if it is how effective it is in a climate of significant welfare cuts.

Supporters of the RNR argue the approach '... does not vary by ethnicity, history of violence or community/custodial setting' (Andrews and Dowden, 2006) but add the caveats that programme fidelity is key to ensuring effectiveness (see Chapter 6).

The rationale for risk-based assessment

Collecting information, analysing it and using it as the basis to make plans for the future appears straightforward and simple, but assessment is not uncontentious. The information that we seek to gather, record and then value or judge important, forms the basis of assessment. In the UK, within the YJS and the CJS, risk-based, actuarial assessments have, since the Crime and Disorder Act (CDA) (1998) had the most value placed upon them. Thus the whole of the current YJS in England and Wales is premised on the notion of risk-based assessment; the forms used for assessment are derived from and predicated on the notions of risk and that is what they record and measure.

In other European countries risk-based assessments do not form the basis of assessment for young people who have committed an offence and the proposed introduction of such forms of assessment is contentious (Coussee et al., 2009). Welfare principles are more common in European social work with young offenders and are strongly defended; assessment may therefore be more similar to the Common Assessment Framwork (CAF). As we saw in Chapter 3, however, there is no definitive evidence that either welfare or justice systems offer better outcomes for young people and within the UK it is accepted that risk-based assessments are not uncontentious (Haines and Case, 2008: Ballucci, 2008):

> discussion about assessment practice can be a reflection of wider debates about the direction of penal policy and the nature of the youth justice system. Assessment practice in a risk-based system may look quite different to practice in a more welfare-oriented system, and there will also be differences of opinion about the relative merits of various methods of assessment ... These are complex issues that cannot be resolved by a simple appeal to statistical data ...
>
> (Youth Justice Board, 2008)

The commissioning and adoption of a new risk-based form of assessment by the YJB in 1998 has formed the foundation to one of the most methodologically driven forms of social work practice in the UK on a large, state scale. The intention was to ensure 'a common framework for assessment practice within the new multi-disciplinary YOTs ...' (Baker, 2004: 70) and bring consistency to a new and emerging partnership form of multi-professional and multi-agency working (Chapter 3). Standardized forms of assessment were also adopted within broader professional social work practice and thus within children's services, the CAF was introduced along with the Every Child Matters (ECM) agenda (2004); both incorporated the common themes of inter-agency, inter-professional and inter-disciplinary practice (Chapters 3 and 4). These forms of assessments and information sharing also sought to maximize emerging practice such as computerized systems. The CAF was designed to capture a wide range of data and is usually said to have been informed by ecological, holistic forms of assessment; and although it has many features in common with Asset it is more easily described as a structured form of assessment, rather than an actuarial one.

Forms of assessment remain an emerging area of study regarding effectiveness and the YJB is once again engaging in this discussion about developing assessment practice and perhaps no longer using Asset; the theoretical background to the discussions are informed by notions of managerial, clinical and social work practice in a 'modern' age (Teli, 2011; Gray et al., 2010; Baker, 2007; Shlonsky and Wagner, 2005). A telling feature will be how costly it will be to introduce such changes in a climate of retrenchment.

Asset when it was launched as part of the YJB approach was new and exciting. It was a research-informed and methodologically driven approach to assessment, seen to be rigorous and measurable, underpinned by evidence. It was anticipated that this new form of assessment should indicate the appropriate intervention and intensity in line with the RNR principles, and that it would be clear what was intended and what the outcomes should be. It was expected to be different and to counter previous concerns about assessments that had been found to lack clarity, with the issues requiring assistance undetermined and no apparent reason for the interventions proffered.

In addition, risk-based or actuarial assessment could be seen to be free from individual bias because the same criteria were applied to each person. In the past there had been concern that individual assessments were discriminatory and there was research that showed how assessments and recommendations regarding the types and levels of intervention were influenced by sexism and racism (Cook and Hudson, 1993). Nonetheless, some would argue that the way risk assessments are formed, the factors which they measure, are in themselves biased or discriminatory, because they do not separate structural factors from individual or agentic ones (Garside, 2009; Ballucci, 2008). This may be due in part to their theoretical basis with psychology favouring individualistic explanations, rather than the structural or policy-focused analysis that might emerge from sociology or social policy theorists. However, prospective, longitudinal research in the Edinburgh Study (Smith, 2004: 208) has given credence to structural factors and class-based discrimination. Smith found that social class was not in itself a predictor of offending, but that 'boys from lower class backgrounds were more likely to come into contact with the police than others, a fact not explained in full by their involvement in delinquency'.

Assessment in the YJS: Asset

The basis of assessment in the YJS is a single actuarial form called Asset. It has, as discussed above, been developed to reflect common factors (or 'risk factors') that research has shown to be common to many young people who come into contact with the YJS and/or who offend (Farrington, 1996). These risk factors are grouped into areas known as 'domains' within Asset (Chapter 4). Most commonly the social worker undertakes an assessment of a young person and recommends a disposal, or way forward – the recommendation may be to take no further action or intervention.

Asset specifically seeks information about the following areas:

- offending behaviour
- living arrangements;
- family and personal relationships;
- education, training and employment;
- neighbourhood;
- lifestyle;
- substance use;
- physical health;
- emotional and mental health;
- perception of self and others;
- thinking and behaviour;
- attitudes to offending;
- motivation to change;
- positive factors;
- indicators of vulnerability;
- indicators of serious harm to others.

Asset seeks to build a picture about the young person by collecting the information about the areas listed above. It has key areas including a 'core profile' and it gives detailed guidance about what is meant by each. One of the areas which Arnull et al. (2005) found youth justice (YJ) practitioners did not know how to use properly and appropriately was the section that is narrative and is intended to provide a detailed summary of the offence committed. The detailed guidance on this section now states that the person undertaking the assessment should consider:

Reasons and motives

These are often linked, but are not necessarily the same. 'Reasons' can include the external events or circumstances which act as triggers for an offence and factors which act as disinhibitors. 'Motives' tend to be more internal and personal (e.g. attitudes, beliefs and desires . . . the apparent absence of any reason or motive for offending could be significant. Seemingly random or unpredictable behaviour may cause considerable concern.

The guidance has therefore directly sought to address the issues raised.

Asset must be completed for all young people subject to:

- bail supervision and support;
- a request for a court report (pre-sentence report and specific sentence report);
- community disposals during the assessment, quarterly review and closure stages;
- custodial sentences at the assessment, transfer to the community and closure stages. Specific Asset forms are available for those receiving Final Warnings.
  (Youth Justice Board, 2000)

As we have already discussed, in order to make a full assessment you will need to interview the young person and their family, obtain information from others and form judgements about the factors that affect the young person's offending behaviour. Establishing a relationship with the young person will therefore be central to the assessment and you will need to use all of your social work skills and methods to do this. Asset simply gives a structure for recording and analysing information but does not say how you should conduct an interview and nor should it form the basis or structure for the interview – it is about you gathering and assembling the appropriate information over time with the relevant parties. Within the YOT you may also need to liaise with those with specialist knowledge to gain their advice and assistance; for example, regarding health issues, education, training and employment (ETE) or substance use/advice.[1] National Standards are quite specific and comprehensive in the minimum standards set and state that each assessment should include:

- an interview with the child or young person;
- an interview with the parents/carers (unless the young person is over 16 years old and not in contact with their parents/carers);
- a review of existing assessments, court or other reports, previous convictions, and so on.
- information from other agencies, such as social services, health, education, housing/ accommodation providers, relevant voluntary sector organizations, and so on.

Asset guidance also says:

You are expected to give details in the evidence box of the problems and needs that you have identified through the preceding tick-box questions in the section. This is important because it shows the basis for your decisions and judgements. It also enables you to explain the complexity of a young person's situation.
(Youth Justice Board, 2008)

Again this is something we know did not occur in the past and is clearly an attempt to improve practice; the intention appears to be that by explaining the importance it will increase practitioner understanding and compliance. Where there are gaps in information National Standards require that this is fully explained and accounted for.

The Asset can therefore be seen to meet the expectations social workers would have about conducting a comprehensive assessment regarding a young person; what is more unusual or contentious is the emphasis that is then placed on how this information is used. Thus, another area that the Asset guidance focuses on is making intelligible the actuarial scoring regarding predicting future offending and establishing criminogenic needs (rather than welfare ones: see Chapter 4). This was also an area that earlier studies on YJ practice found practitioners did not understand (Arnull et al., 2005), but as you can see it is very clearly linked to the risk factors' research and highlights the importance of practitioners being cognizant of research findings. Thus the guidance now says when giving a rating about the likelihood of further offending and the domain area of Asset (i.e. family, education) the practitioner should think:

- Was this issue linked to past offending? If 'yes', do you think it is more, less or equally significant now?
- Has this issue a direct or an indirect link with his/her offending?
- Is this issue always relevant to his/her offending behaviour or only on certain occasions?
- Is the effect on offending behaviour likely to be immediate or over a longer period?
- Is this issue problematic enough to lead to offending by itself or is it only likely to contribute to offending behaviour when certain other conditions exist?

(Youth Justice Board, 2008)

The extent to which a section is associated with the likelihood of further offending is rated on a 0–4 scale with '0 Not associated at all . . . 4 Very strongly associated . . .'. It is possible to see how an assessment structured to focus on risk of offending (rather than welfare need for example) can be very difficult for a social worker and it has much in common with those working in other areas; for example, mental health settings. The assessment is clearly risk-focused and actuarial; as we discussed earlier, however, there are social work skills and methods that ensure you can bring your values and ethics to bear and ensure an appropriate and just assessment. Furthermore, because the only justification for engagement with the young person is that they have committed an offence (or are said to have done so regarding bail), it is not inappropriate that this should form the basis and focus of the assessment.

Thus, although Asset is a comprehensive assessment in its scope, it does focus its questions towards offending and the potential for the young person to cause harm. Nonetheless, it should also identify areas for potential/actual harm to the young person. However, the guidance that focuses on 'recent' events and suggests workers 'may if they wish' record in dialogue boxes previous harms, substance using or offending parents, it is likely to mean that this relevant information may be overlooked in ongoing assessments undertaken by busy practitioners. As we saw earlier, the evidence regarding previous victimization of young people in the YJS would indicate that these are important areas which should not be 'overlooked'. Additionally, earlier studies indicated that these boxes often remained incomplete and staff did not use them to build depth and history into their assessments (Arnull et al., 2005); as a result the roundedness of the young person's life and experiences were missed. An ecological/holistic assessment is not therefore undertaken as a matter of course, although the guidance really seeks to lead the practitioner to do so; a social worker should appreciate the importance of compiling a full and complete picture. However, as we also know YJ work can be busy and pressured and Asset can all too often become a static document with information cut and pasted, rather than the dynamic document that was intended.

The 'what do you think' section of Asset does offer a real opportunity for young people to input into their own assessment and thereby affect what the assessment records about them, interventions (or not) that are planned and proposed (or not) and thus the overall outcome. However, we know that this section is not currently well used in YOTs and further that many young people in the YJS will have had past experiences of abuse, disaffection from school, disruption to housing and living arrangements and may have been in care – the potential for the young person to distrust the social worker (or YOT worker) is therefore considerable. Arnull et al. (2005) found that the most important factor for engaging young offenders with lengthy experiences of offending and social work interventions was the relationship they built up with the adult responsible for their intervention; the report noted that for some of the young people this was the only positive or non-abusive relationship the young person had experienced with an adult. The YJB's report on engagement has subsequently added further weight to this view (Mason and Prior, 2008). It is therefore probable that the 'what do you think' section of Asset may need to be repeated over time with the young person to enable them to reflect more accurately the 'real' situation in their lives as they build trust in the person with whom they are working.

Many of the young people with whom you engage in the YJS will have disclosed personal and distressing information to other adults before and can therefore on occasions seem disassociated from doing so during the assessment process; as a result an erroneous assumption can be formed that they are 'not bothered' by past events. It is important to recall that they may have disclosed information that led to no action, or change, or improvement in their life and therefore feel despondent, or negative about the potential benefits of engaging with the social worker. Alternatively, they may have disclosed information that led to a serious interruption or disruption in their life/living arrangements. Young people who have been victimized and/or had negative experiences, may themselves be hard to engage, difficult and not characters with whom it is easy to empathize. As a social worker in the YJS you must recognize the potential for this and the possibility that you may not always find it easy to empathize with your most difficult clients. The case review of Aliyah Ismail (BBC, 1999) demonstrated that the risks to her were improperly understood. Professionals (including social workers) did not listen to what she was saying, or act to protect her. She frequently ran away (a consistent factor indicating possible abuse), but this fact was used as the basis to control her, rather than care for her. Aspects that were highlighted were that social workers did not properly assess or listen to her, or plan interventions that met her needs; her apparent unwillingness to engage appears to have been interpreted as her 'failure'.

Social workers undertaking assessments with young people in the YJS should therefore see the assessment process as an ongoing one; approach the subject matter sensitively; be open to other ways of describing behaviour, living arrangements, relationships and lifestyle choices, which may appear to the young person more acceptable, or in their view may safeguard them from unwarranted intrusion or offers of assistance that they do not welcome. A social worker working within the YJS must remember that many of the young people they meet may in the past have been a 'child in need', have experienced a disruptive childhood, negative experiences, bereavement and loss or may at that time be struggling with transition from childhood to adulthood with little guidance, stability or few positive role models (Chapters 1 and 4).

As social workers we should practice in an anti-oppressive (AO) way and this also means remaining open to the possibility that there is 'nothing wrong'; we should not seek to pathologize 'naughty', deviant, anti-social or criminal behaviour. Research by Arnull and Eagle (2009) indicated that for a substantial number of girls and young women in the YJS there were few explanatory factors for their behaviour other than that on occasions they got into disputes and sometimes fights with other girls. For these girls, YOTs' staff assessed that there were issues of anger management, use of alcohol and high levels of low self-esteem – these factors would however be consistent with those for a very large numbers of girls and young women (especially adolescents and teenagers) who have not become involved with the YJS and there is nothing very much 'wrong' that they will not learn to control or grow out of.

Furthermore, there is a body of evidence indicating that for many young people it is better when social workers, and others, do not intervene (Dugmore et al., 2006; self-report studies; Smith, 2004).

Additionally, research (particularly related to adults) suggests that based on the same sort of information some groups (especially women) are particularly likely to be offered interventions, especially social care ones, which problematize their behaviour or lead to the social control of their lives; whereas a man would not have experienced that level of intrusion or pathologizing of their behaviour. Similarly, other groups will not be offered social care interventions, even where the information indicates they should be. These findings have been particularly correlated with race and especially black (African-Caribbean) men, who were less likely to be assessed as needing care or support leading to higher rates of imprisonment (Cook and Hudson, 1993).

Attitudes, assumptions, values, discrimination and bias can play a part in assessment and more proscriptive forms such as Asset go some way to ameliorating the potential for discrimination, because they ensure consistency in the factors considered as part of an assessment and ask for scoring mechanisms and evidence. Nonetheless, the assessment process is one that is essentially about professional judgement, and thus social workers undertaking assessment should guard against allowing bias and discriminatory thinking to pervade their assessments. They should remain alive to the possibility that nothing is required and that the best outcome might be for no further form of involvement.

Onset

As Wilson et al. (2008) outline, assessment is for a range of purposes and Onset was developed as an assessment tool for young people who are considered to be at risk of offending, and anti-social behaviour. It was developed by the YJB in order to enhance their 'prevention agenda'. It may therefore be used to assess young people within a

YISP setting, although CAFs will also be completed by staff within that setting or a referral may be made directly to children's services.

The Common Assessment Framework (CAF)

There was and is, therefore, a clear rationale for the way in which assessment is undertaken in the YJS. But it is important that as a social worker within the YJS you understand that other forms of assessment are used by social workers and these are usually derived from a theoretically informed basis. They may incorporate welfare principles (and most commonly do) and the assessment may follow a common, prescribed framework imposed on, or adopted by, the assessor (actuarial or structured), or the form of assessment might follow the individual practice of a given social worker/other professional (clinical).

For those working with children and young people in England and Wales who are in contact with the YJS, the next most likely form of 'other' assessment that you will encounter is the CAF. This is a tool used by all those assessing children and young people in contact with the social care system and it uses a different approach from Asset. As a result the YJB gives guidance to those working within the YJS about when and how this form of assessment should be used. The CAF was deliberately designed to be able to be used by a wide range of practitioners and to be able to be 'added' to by different groups at different points in an assessment cycle, without the need for a wholly new assessment; like Asset it was piloted prior to its implementation with practitioners to get feedback on its ease of use, applicability, and so on. However, in practice, anecdotal evidence suggests it is rare for other professionals, including social workers in YOTs, to complete or add to a CAF. The reasoning is that if need is demonstrated, a social worker from a children and families team would need to redo the CAF in order to ascertain whether or not the eligibility criteria for that service were met. Thus practice has become resources- or rationing-led, although this is in itself a waste of resources. This is interesting, because CAF was influenced by a partnership approach to social policy and social work that was both popular and increasingly common in social policy/care settings from the late 1990s. The development of CAF was also influenced by and based on the knowledge that previous assessments undertaken by different professional groups were rarely shared or used when new assessments were undertaken; it was therefore a key part of the impetus for the development of the CAF to ensure that it would be a usable, common and shared tool for assessment. Thus, where a CAF is required, National Standards Guidance (YJB, 2000) states that it should be completed by a social worker in a YOT in line with local agreements that are in place. Because local social services teams provide the social workers to the multidisciplinary YOT they should be cognizant of thresholds for services and should therefore be able to undertake the assessment; in practice, however, it would seem that barriers have, in the main, remained impervious to developments of this sort.

Pre-Sentence Reports (PSRs)

A PSR is completed on a young person who appears in court in connection with a criminal offence which they admit, or for which they have been found guilty and for whom a court has then requested one. The court must obtain a PSR, or a Specific Sentence Report (SSR) from the YOT before imposing a custodial or community sentence (s. 156 Criminal Justice Act 2003). The report should include an assessment of the nature and seriousness of the offence, and its impact on the victim (see Chapter 1). A PSR is defined in s. 158 Criminal Justice Act 2003 as a report which:

(a) with a view to assisting the court in determining the most suitable method of dealing with an offender, is made or submitted by an appropriate officer, and

(b) contains information as to such matters, presented in such manner, as may be prescribed by rules made by the Secretary of State.

The PSR should be shown to the offender or their legal representative (s. 159(2)(a) Criminal Justice Act 2003) and where the young person is under 18, the court must also give a copy to their parent or guardian (s. 159(2)(b)).

Clearly, in order to be able to prepare the report for court the social worker must complete an assessment. The method for doing so will be strongly influenced by the approaches and methods that underpin the whole of the YJS as discussed above.

Other forms of assessment

Not all assessments follow a preset formula or use a prescribed format. Nonetheless, assessment is and/or should be grounded in a theoretical approach and the practitioner should have a clear idea of the reasons for, justification and purpose of the assessment and what the range of outcomes might be. Different social work methods will influence the type of assessment undertaken and it is probable that these will guide the focus towards different elements of a person's life. Thus an assessment undertaken by a social worker whose work is oriented towards a cognitive behavioural, psycho-analytic or task-focused form of intervention will be more likely to see different aspects of a person's life and previous experiences as more or less relevant. A person's history and in particular their development as a child is more likely to be given greater prominence or consideration by a psycho-dynamic practitioner, whereas a cognitive behavioural therapist may be more interested in the way a person makes decisions, forms judgements, plans and takes action.

It is argued by some (Foyer Foundation for example: Carlin, undated) that most current forms of assessment seek to 'count' or measure the negative aspects of a person's life; they argue instead for a form of assessment that counts the positive things in someone's life, or their strengths and achievements; this is referred to as 'strengths-based assessment' (see earlier this chapter). Although it has its supporters within social work and the voluntary sector, and Dugmore et al. (2007) suggest it allows for engagement of the service user, there have been few evaluations of its effectiveness. There is no obvious reason why a strengths-based approach must of necessity engage the service user more than other forms of assessment; unless for example a 'diagnostic' or clinical approach is being taken in which the assessor will then 'dispense' treatment in accordance with their professional 'diagnosis', but this type of approach is rare in social work because of the possibility for exclusion of the service user's views and thus sits less comfortably with social work values and ethics.

While most forms of assessment seek to construct a full picture of a person and their life, some have this concept at the heart of their theoretical and/or practice approach. A number of theoretical approaches used within a social work setting do this; one such approach is systems theory that has been currently popularized and discussed with regard to organizational responses to working with children and young people at risk of significant harm is the Munroe Report (2011). Additionally, ecological theory (Brofenbrenner, 1979) seeks to construct an understanding of the person, their community, family; namely, the 'ecological system' within which they operate and function. This approach is popular in continental Europe where community-based approaches and assessments also continue to be more common (e.g. social pedagogy). These types of approaches consider factors such as family members, school, peers/friends/siblings, housing, the community, and so on.

This information is often displayed diagrammatically and shared with the service user to allow the practitioner and the service user to decide on the area(s) of focus. It can also be used to 'predict' the future, because past patterns or behaviours are considered and can be built into the pattern, system or diagram that is constructed. The service user can themselves be included in the drawing/constructing of the system or framework and this can form a method of intervention in the early stages of assessment. Although different in origination, within the UK, some approaches to Family Group Conferencing use a similar methodology, seeking to draw the person and their family directly into thinking about the issues and considering solutions as part of the assessment process; it is used in some areas as a method of children and families work and within the YJS (Chapter 9).

Methods of assessment that seek to involve the service user can be empowering and successful at engaging young people who may be anxious or unwilling to engage in protracted discussion, seemingly without purpose, about their 'problems'. Ecological forms of assessment, life maps and 'snakes' and other forms of visual/word-based assessment were in my experience particularly effective in engaging young people in communication and dialogue that they were able to direct and contribute to. The service user can 'see' and participate in their own assessment, they can make connections between aspects of, or activities in, their own lives and this can help them to 'uncover' and make explicit issues and difficulties.

Coming from a similar perspective is the 'exchange model' in which the 'service user is identified as the expert in their own life' (Wilson et al., 2008: 287) encouraging an exchange of information between practitioner and service user, which then forms the basis of the assessment. The model seeks to empower the service user to participate in the assessment process and it is possible to adopt this model within a risk-based framework: within Asset this is facilitated in the service user section where the young person gets to say what they think. However, as Wilson et al. (2008: 279) also note, this method is not without its critics and it is possible for social workers to 'overestimate service users' abilities to identify solutions to their difficulties' and to 'underestimate or deny their own level of professional expertise'.

The key factor in engaging and empowering the service user is for the social work practitioner to use the tools that are available to them to practise in a reflective, AO and AD way and assess the ability of the young person to engage and then ensure they are enabled to do so appropriately.

Service user engagement in the process of assessment

All forms of assessment should seek to involve and engage the young person and where appropriate their family/carers and the section above has sought to make explicit how this might be achieved within the YJ setting. As a social worker it is also important that you are aware of the language you use and ensure that the young person and relevant others understand what is being said to them, what is being asked and that what they say is accurately recorded. This is can be challenging within a legal framework where the language is often obfuscated and difficult. Additionally, assessments can be misleading because respondents/service users do not want to answer questions or use the terminology given for a variety of reasons. Arnull et al. (2007) for example found that homelessness was seriously underestimated by practitioners because of the language that they used when conducting the assessment. Young people had much higher thresholds of dispossession when talking about homelessness than did practitioners and equated homelessness with negative stereotypes that they did not want applied to them. They may also have understood the risks of being seen to be homeless in the criminal justice system (CJS) in which homelessness has often led to a greater risk of incarceration.

Additionally, practitioners have been found to assess children and young people as not having needs that the worker knows they do not have the resources to meet. For example, in the same piece of research, Arnull et al. (2007) found that YOT workers 'underscored' housing-related needs when they knew there was no available or suitable provision. Assessment should not be guided by what the practitioner/social worker knows to be available. This is often referred to in the literature as resource-led, rather than needs-led, assessment. Interventions are the next step and we would argue that as social workers we should not be jumping ahead to assess need on the basis of provision we know to be available; for example, as we have seen, social work ethics explicitly argue for social workers to campaign for the resources required to meet need. Current social work practice offers a challenge to this view with 'thresholds' and eligibility-based assessments. Nonetheless in line with ethics and values as social workers we could make use of collated and anonymized data, collected as a result of assessments, to argue for resources and provision.

There is growing concern also about the learning needs and abilities of young people who find themselves subject to assessment by YOTs and their ability to participate; reviews of the way in which assessment is conducted in the YOTs is currently influenced in part by this concern (Teli, 2011).

Professional practice, theory and assessment

It is important that social workers adopt a proactive approach to their own professional perspective and ensure that this remains up to date; as discussed, there have been very public criticisms that as a profession social work has failed to do this in the past (SWRB, 2010; Munroe 2011). Arnull et al. (2005) and Baker (2005) found social workers and other YOT practitioners undertaking assessments and planning interventions across England and Wales who did not really understand the empirical research basis of the assessment tool they were using. Because of this they did not really know how to apply or use certain tools contained within it effectively, namely scoring. This suggested that practitioners needed to equip themselves with the skills they needed as reflective and proactive practitioners (SCIE, 2005). Subsequently, work has focused on looking at the reliability and use of Asset by practitioners (XJB 2008) and increasing practitioner understanding; and as a result guidance has become clearer and more refined.

It is important to remember that at the basis of any assessment are the issues considered in Chapter 3: good communication skills that are AO and AD and reflective, theory-informed practice that upholds social work values and allows a relationship to be formed. The Children's Society 'Good Childhood Blog' highlights the importance of forming relationships: 'Our research into young people's well-being shows how important relationships are to young people, not only their relationships with friends and family, but also with adults in their community' (The Children's Society, 2011).

Social work values, assessment and social policy

The potential power of assessment is to ensure that it leads appropriately into justifiable intervention. In so doing it also has the potential to enable social workers to demonstrate whether or not they 'do things differently or more expertly' (Rees and Wallace, 1982) than people who are not social workers. Rees and Wallace outline the perennial problem for social work, which is to clearly explain what it does and the difference it can make; thus, that it produces better outcomes.

The difficulty for social work as a profession in articulating what it does, how it does it and why that makes a difference, has continued and in some senses the problems and issues that have beset social work in recent years following the Baby Peter case and reviews of social work practice and leadership have reflected this difficulty: that the profession has failed to speak more widely to service users, government and the public about the difference it can make and how it has done this (Munroe, 2011).

Social workers have considerable potential power over the lives of the people they are asked to work with: with children and families this includes the power to recommend removal of the child from the home, with the disabled it may be about access to care and assistance, with the elderly it might involve substantial control and influence over their access to their income and where they live. Within the YJS the social worker will make recommendations that might involve a young person's liberty, access to programmes across the spectrum of health and social care and housing and education: the potential power and influence of social workers is therefore considerable. Given this the assessments that social workers make must be accurate, clear, intelligible and justifiable. Arguably, social workers should be able to demonstrate the evidence base of their assessments; why is their judgement more justifiable, accurate and worth following than any that might be made by any other profession or member of the public? There are considerable debates that rage among social work academics about the nature of evidence. These debates often focus on the privileging of certain forms of evidence/data; with some (Sheldon, 2001) arguing that large-scale quantitative data has more to tell us than smaller-scale qualitative research. However, this is often to misunderstand the value of qualitative research; good research should ensure that the methods used are applicable to the question in hand. Qualitative research is designed to answer process questions: why and how did something occur, what did people think, how did they feel? It is also designed to understand the situational nature of behaviour and can uncover attitudes and responses and help to understand individual or group responses. It is derived from anthropology and sociology and can be used to answer questions about policy, organizations, groups or individuals. Quantitative research is designed to test a hypothesis, it is experimental and is asking if something 'works'; for example a treatment/intervention. It is associated with hierarchies of evidence and uses terms such as 'gold standard'; it is based on positivistic methods and is used to answer questions about groups. Both types of research have their own valuable role to play and this should not be ignored.

Social workers should be able to refer to the evidence that underpins their assessments and be able to indicate identifiable and projected impacts in given circumstances from planned interventions. Were social workers to do this regularly it might be more intelligible to service users why particular recommendations are being made; other professional groups and the public might also see what social work was bringing to the table and social workers might also be better placed to evidence the need for social justice.

There has been considerable criticism of what are often portrayed as increasingly managerial and depoliticized systems (Davies, 2002; Muncie, 2009; Fecley and Simon, 1996) but as discussed above the information can be used by social work professionals to influence and campaign for resources and change. Research indicates that there is increasing sophistication at a multi-agency partnership level and that some are finding ways to use the information available to them to plan and influence provision that meets local need (Arnull, 2008).

Outcomes of assessment

The YJB's emphasis at the assessment stage is overly focused on outcomes (see YJB, 2008) and this distorts the process. The purpose of assessment may be to help someone make sense of their own situation and see pathways towards goals and while these may be 'outcomes', these may be short term, or longer term, and they may be part of a therapeutic process. The remit for the social worker in the assessment process in the YJS is to focus on and consider the following three outcomes:

- **Offending/reoffending:** the likelihood that a young person will become involved in offending or commit further offences.
- **Serious harm to others:** the risk that a young person might inflict serious harm on other people (e.g. serious violent or sexual offences).
- **Vulnerability:** the possibility that a young person might be harmed in some way, either because of their own behaviour or through the actions or omissions of others.

(YJB, 2008: 11)

It is essential that as a social worker you use your clinical skills and professional values to ensure you are looking at the whole person in their holistic situation and ensuring therefore that the assessment captures the full range of possibilities and is not utilitarian, focused only on the 'outcomes' that are available and preset. Some research suggests however that practitioners are not making the most of the opportunities to do this and often their reports lack analysis and 'only provide a description or repetition of facts recorded elsewhere' (YJB, 2008: 23; Baker, 2007; Shlonsky and Wagner, 2005). To act in this way would not be in accordance with social work's professional ethics and values. But research by Baker (2007), which compared assessment by social workers and YJ practitioners, showed a tendency to emphasize or focus on particular aspects and not to look at the person being assessed in their whole context, thus missing key areas. However, work by Shlonsky and Wagner (2005) that reviewed evidence on actuarial, consensus and clinical decision-making found there was clear evidence that actuarial assessment was on the whole more accurate and comprehensive because it forced the practitioner into a wider consideration. The evidence suggests therefore that actuarial assessment does not per se lead to limited assessments and that these can occur regardless of the form of assessment undertaken. Once again therefore it highlights the need for proactive, reflective practitioners to take a holistic and professional approach. As Shlonsky and Wagner (2005: 420) argue:

> A risk classification . . . is not an infallible prediction, nor is it a substitute for the exercise of sound professional judgment . . . Appropriate use in the field requires that workers understand how actuarial risk assessments work, know the limitations of the estimates they make, and receive the training and policy guidance necessary to employ them effectively in the field.

The YJB says that YOT reports will be balanced, impartial, timely, focused, free from discriminatory language and stereotypes, verified, factually accurate, intelligible to the child or young person and their parents/carers. In addition they should provide the required level of information and analysis to enable sentencers to make informed decisions about sentencing options. This is what you are expected to produce. To do so requires the following:

- considerable analytical skills;
- the ability to synthesize information from a variety of different sources;
- make it intelligible and applicable to as diverse an audience as a young person, who may also have low levels of literacy, little interest, but upon whom it may have considerable impact, and the judiciary and legal representatives who will have high levels of literacy, a focused and critical interest but upon whom (in real terms) it will have little impact.

This skill base is given much less attention than the debates about the relative effectiveness of different forms of assessment. In part this may be because even when documents, such as the YJB's 'Assessment, Planning Interventions and Supervision' (2008), say they are written for practitioners not an academic or research audience, they are clearly written with the latter in mind. Furthermore, two factors affect the impact that social workers have on the multidisciplinary environment, which is the YJS, one is that it is a multidisciplinary setting and thus there are a number of voices and professional perspectives to be heard; the second is that as a profession social work has not to date been good at making its voice heard and asserting its professional perspective (SWRB, 2010; Munroe, 2011). In YJB (2008: 13–14) there is a brief acknowledgement that:

> Although the evidence indicates that . . . actuarial predictions tend to be more accurate than those based purely on clinical judgement, it is important to remember that different methods are required for different types of risk. To give an example, clinical assessment is still important in the assessment of rare events such as very serious offences where actuarial tools have been shown to be less accurate. In such cases, the use of 'structured clinical assessment' (i.e. a framework of key factors to consider) can be most useful.

This is also picked up in the review by Shlonsky and Wagner (2005: 421) who draw out that actuarial assessment cannot replace clinical aspects of assessment, nor can they: '. . . engage the family in cooperative case planning, assess their functioning, establish case plan goals, or choose treatment interventions . . .'.

And perhaps this is the place where we as social workers in the YJS should be focusing: on aspects of good, ethical, relationship-based practice that we bring, working to enhance and develop actuarial forms of assessment (Gray et al., 2010). The YJB guidance describes the absence of critical and analytical thinking in assessments in the YJB and children and families work without really addressing how practitioners might overcome this (YJB, 2008: 23). The issue is that critical and analytical skills are not being utilized and these are the basis of professional social work.

The Inspectorate of Youth Offending (IYO) and Criminal Justice Joint Inspection CJJI (IYO/CJJI: 2011) reviewed offending behaviour, health and education programmes (Chapter 6) and found that good 'Likelihood of Reoffending' assessments were completed at the start of supervision but these rarely included all the elements of work to be undertaken. This is congruent with earlier research (Arnull et al., 2005), which found that assessments were frequently not updated, nor the reasons for intervention and anticipated outcomes clearly specified. Social work values and ethics talk about empowerment of the service user but it is difficult for people to be empowered if they do not know why something is being proposed, and do not have access to updated information that outlines the progress they have (or have not) made. Currently, simplified forms of assessment and reviews of progress or the impact of the intervention are being developed that seek to engage the service user and enable them to also consider change/progress (e.g. 'Star' assessments used by Coram).

As discussed risk-based assessments work on the basis of statistical probabilities and this can be a blunt tool, which is good at generalizations about groups, but not specific about individuals.[2] Thus, actuarial assessment tools are only as good as the person using them; social work skills are essential, especially where need or risk is greatest. The success of an assessment in terms of the 'outcomes' on which the YJB places so much emphasis depends on the clinical skills of the practitioner: the relationship that is constructed with the young person (Shlonsky and Wagner, 2005), the importance of multidisciplinary working (IYO/CJJI, 2011; Burnett and Appleton, 2004) and the ability to gather, critically analyse and synthesize the information for a diverse audience making a defensible recommendation that others are minded to accept.

EXERCISES

1   Take a sheet of paper and divide it in half. On one half write down the 'positive' things about risk-based actuarial assessment, including social policy that supports/promotes it. On the other half write down all the 'negative' things about it, including social policy that has promoted other forms of assessment.

2   Using the case study scenario on page x follow assessment 'steps' and answer: who is concerned about what and why; what are the risks; what are the positives/strengths; who should you contact/speak to; what is your hypothesis about what is going on; with whom and how can you verify/disprove this; what are some possible outcomes; what are the advantages/disadvantages of each outcome?

Notes

1   Although this section is reworded it follows the format of the YJB guidance to ensure it is congruent with it.
2   See the discussion re 'types' of research and evidence-based practice (EBP).

6

Intervention

LEARNING OUTCOMES

By the end this chapter you should be able to:

*   Appreciate the range and type of interventions within the youth justice system (YJS).
*   Reflect upon interventions within the YJS and how they can be considered through the lens of Anti-Oppressive (AO) and Anti-Discriminatory (AD) practice.

In this chapter we explore 'what works' in terms of evidence-based and effective practice with offenders. We explore the interventions available or prescribed within National Standards, local boundaries and local authority budgets. We discuss whether these interventions are service- or needs-led and tailored to meet the potential requirements of the young person or the constraints of the local authority purse. The potential for these approaches to be oppressive or to discriminate and further marginalize certain groups of young people is examined.

Intervening

The YJB (2008: 5) states that:

> Assessment, planning interventions and supervision (APIS) are essential elements of practice with young people at all stages of the youth justice system – from early intervention programmes, through to Final Warnings, community supervision and custodial sentences.

It says that interventions should be planned on the basis of:

- identifying level and intensity of intervention required
- defining relevant and clear targets for action.

(YJB, 2008)

Further interventions within Youth Offending Teams (YOTs) should be delivered in accordance with three principles: risk, needs and responsivity (Chapter 5). This means that the intervention should be matched to the young person's likelihood of reoffending, their criminogenic needs and their learning style, motivation and personal experiences. As discussed in Chapter 7, interventions within the YJS are, however, now subject to the Scaled Approach and thus identifying the level and intensity of supervision is key to what is subsequently planned and agreed. The basis of the model that the YJS uses is driven by a desire to provide '. . . a foundation for practice and a framework within which specific interventions are most likely to have a positive effect' (YJB 2008). The underpinning belief is founded on an acceptance of risk-based, actuarial work that, as we discussed Chapter 5, is the basis of assessment in the YJS; thus there is a consistency of theory to the YJS model. The premise is that interventions are most effective when targeted to meet criminogenic needs and risk (IYO/ CJJI, 2011). These conceptions have been powerful more generally within the criminal justice system (CJS) in the UK and are clearly linked to evidence-based practice undertaken within the probation service. Much of the work within the adult system has been informed by psychologists who developed group work programmes, which they said were more effective when targeted on criminogenic need and when delivered by trained staff who were compliant with/or ensured programme 'integrity'; that is, that they delivered the programme to a specified framework and in a specified way. These sorts of groups have been used substantially within the adult system, for example, with drink drivers. In some ways this has been an interesting development and leads to the consideration of the trajectory of different professional groups.

Prior to the 1980s, probation officers were of high status, mainly male and allowed a considerable degree of professional freedom and responsibility. However, in the 1990s, the training framework changed; there was the impact of considerable welfare cuts, high levels of concern about crime and rising drug use and the 1970s' 'nothing works' attacks on social work, alongside Michael Howard's (the then Home Secretary) now infamous 'prison works' speech. Into this period came the 'what works' agenda linked to evidence-based practice and at the same time psychologists who held up an apparently 'magic wand' of group-based, criminogenic programmes that they described in pseudo-scientific language and evaluated using very particular methodologies; intentionally, or not, they quite carefully controlled both the agenda and the means by which that would be judged (Wilson et al., 2008: 351). The evidence they then presented suggested that certain sorts of programme; for example, cognitive behavioural theory (CBT), devised by their own professional group, would lower recidivism. In turn, the adult CJS bought into many of these programmes at a time of 'marketization' of statutory services. In this case the probation officer appeared downgraded and retrained in many instances to deliver programmes designed by another professional group; subsequently, many of those programmes are now delivered by unqualified staff trained to deliver the programmes with significantly reduced costs.

What psychologists who developed and delivered these programmes also built into them were the concepts of programme integrity and targeting of offender to the 'right' programme; thus when these programmes did not deliver the expected high-level impact on recidivism it could be said that this was the fault of those delivering the programme – that they did not do it 'right' (programme integrity) or that the 'right' sort of offenders were not sent to the programme and thus the 'right' crimino-genic factors were not able to be targeted. CBT-based interventions have been criti-cized because they appear to suggest the method is always right and if benefits are not evidenced it is the fault of human operatives or subjects, not the theory or method. However, the theory and method are meant to impact on human behaviour and although there is some good evidence for CBT in some areas of social work, it has not proved the panacea to recidivism that was promised. Drawing on the knowledge you have gained about research and research evidence, think through what the advantages and disadvantages to a CBT approach might be for social workers. Remember too that this was and is an attempt to introduce a measurement of effectiveness into social care interventions; in so doing it was more explicit and open than had previously been the case for many of the interventions used. And in this it draws on the framework for sound, evidence-based practice in health care and which has been applied to social care (Sackett et al., 1996). Those precepts are difficult for any practitioner to dispute, and they are that practice should be 'conscientious, explicit and judicious'. However, as the SWRB (2010) highlights current social work methods of intervention are often based on intuition, discussions with colleagues and past practice and not consistently on the judicious use of sound knowledge about their appropriateness and effective-ness. If we think back to our discussions of a reflective, service user-focused, ethical basis to social work we cannot think that situation is appropriate. As social workers we need to think about the interventions we use and whether these will truly help the person with whom we are intervening and how well we can demonstrate that.

Interventions delivered within the YJS: social work methods

The groupwork accredited programme within the YJS has not been developed in the same way as in the adult system but some of the same precepts and language is common to both areas; for example: 'a young person may benefit more from a partic-ular group work programme if it is delivered in a context where staff try to engage him/her in a positive relationship and also demonstrate a consistent approach to compliance and enforcement' (YJB, 2008: 7).

However, the reader will note the more hesitant language, the 'may' and the emphasis on the importance of relationship-building. This is congruent with Aaron Beck (Beck with Beck 2011) one of the early exponents of CBT methods but it is a feature that was in the mass introduction of CBT programmes given less emphasis. However, research looking at service user feedback has consistently shown this to be important to them. The YJB does continue to work to an overall ethos of evidence-based practice underpinned by CBT methods, and reports such as the 2011 Inspection Report underline this, discussing treatment integrity, a collaborative approach and naming CBT interventions (IYO/CJJI, 2011: 9). This highlights the continued drive towards these theories and methods within the YJB that influence groupwork programmes, but also the prewritten and suggested 'packages' that are aimed at one-to-one work. It is important for practitioners to ensure that where they are using a 'package' of support that it is delivered utilizing their basic social work skills of communication and relationship-building; this will have a key impact on its 'effectiveness'. The Inspection Report also highlights the Key Elements of Effective Practice (KEEP) guidance that underlines the need for the intervention to be relevant to the young person, their offending and their needs. As we have discussed (Chapter 5) research has found that interventions can be planned on the basis of what exists rather than what the young person needs. Further, Arnull and Eagle (2009) found that while good practice suggested gender-specific interventions were effective with girls, they usually existed only where a practitioner had a specific personal interest and undertook the work in addition to their allocated load; it was rare for additional resources to be directed towards them. While this appeared discriminatory the justification appeared to be that the low and fluctuating number of girls within individual YOTs made it hard to address their specific needs; the research report recommended that 'if gender mainstreaming is to be taken seriously then staff developing and delivering gender-specific programmes require considerably more support . . .' (Arnull and Eagle, 2000: 15).

The basic building blocks that underpin all of the interventions with which social workers are involved are the same as for other social work interventions and use the same methods. Within a YOT they may also provide practical help and support, befriending or mentoring. As we have seen, theory and method influence the assessment process and the subsequent information that is obtained and considered relevant to any forthcoming intervention. Similarly, the methods underpinning the interventions come from the same core theories and as discussed above draw on theoretical and conceptual models that may come from social work or other related fields. Within the YJS there is currently consistency in the methods that underpin assessment and intervention – they are risk-based and actuarial; this is uncommon in social work in the UK and it appears that this is a potentially changing landscape (Teli, 2011). We therefore briefly discuss common social work methods:[1]

Cognitive behavioural interventions have, as we have seen above, been extremely influential in the adult CJS but have impacted upon the YJS too, although in different ways. They are interventions approved by the National Institute for Clinical Excellence (NICE) as the 'talking therapy of choice' on the basis of the 'evidence' they offer for their effectiveness. CBT is based on social learning theory, it is concerned with conscious thought and argues that we behave in ways which we have learned or been conditioned to respond to; through its interventions it seeks to alter the cognitive processes and thus effect change. It has a number of elements such as 'modelling' appropriate behaviour, 'positively reinforcing' required behaviour and the 'extinction' of inappropriate behaviour by ignoring it, 'fading' the intervention out over time to decrease dependency and interrupting or modifying 'negative schemas' to encourage positivity. CBT has been shown to be effective with particular groups and its strengths are in its emphasis on clear assessment and targeted interventions. Critics argue that it can ride roughshod over service users' rights by seeking to alter their thinking patterns without being explicit. And, that because it is based on learning theory and seeks to interrupt old behaviours, it can transgress service users' rights in the way it seeks to control and contain. Finally that it ignores structural inequalities, social policy and other factors outside a person's control and assumes that the issue/problem to be 'fixed' is inherently the service user.

Systems theory is reflected in the mode of tool assessment (Asset), used in the YJS. It is clearly reflected in Common Assessment Frameworks (CAFs), which seek to take a holistic view and appears to be a trajectory which the YJB may follow (Teli, 2011). It is increasingly popular in the UK and popularized via Munroe (2011) and prevalent in European social work. Systems theory is most concerned with social functioning and the 'health' and 'balance' of the 'systems' within which the service user lives. Interventions include some forms of family work (including conferencing although this can be influenced by restorative justice (RJ), multi-agency work, networking and community work, ecological, narrative or life-course work. The Troubled Families Agenda (2012) appears influenced by systemic thinking. Within the YJS the recognition of this approach is evidenced in the inclusion of housing, education and other specialist workers thereby recognizing the 'whole' system of someone's life. Depending on how systems theory is practised it can make explicit the structural factors in someone's life – helping to recognize and bring these into the 'system' to be changed – this would be more common in an ecological or community-focused approach than family therapy for example. By working with an individual, family member(s) and relevant others it can make explicit connections, disjunctions and power imbalances and address strategies to change/challenge these. Because of the way information is collected it is explicit in the inclusion and engagement of the service user and clearly involves them in making decisions about the areas to be worked on/targeted. It draws on an individual's and families' resources and recognizes strengths and resilience. Critics would argue that in identifying so much it can be hard to 'target' key areas, that it is hard to use with non-engaging families and that it can assume an 'equality' of power within a family. Further, because in some forms of systems theory interventions practitioners adopt a 'neutral' stance seeking the 'expertise' of the family to resolve the 'problem', it is argued that there can be a failure to apportion appropriate culpability.

Psychodynamic social work used to be the most common form of social work practice but experienced a considerable period of unpopularity during the 1980s and early 2000s as a response to the 'nothing works' research that suggested it did not impact on or help people to change their behaviour. More recently it is experiencing resurgence and some of this work has been developed in the CJS in particular using attachment theory with adult offenders (Ansbro, 2008). It is not used explicitly in the YJS although some practitioners may be influenced by it or practise it in a one-to-one setting; however, concepts that are integral to it will be familiar to most. Concepts in psychodynamic work include a view that there are both 'conscious' and 'unconscious' states of being, an openness to emotional experience, theories of development and maturation and their effect on the adult self, such as attachment theory, engagement, transference, counter-transference and endings. The language has become ingrained in much of everyday discourse even where it is not used by a psychodynamic practitioner. The benefits of this approach can be to assist the practitioner to do more than complete concrete tasks as it emphasizes the emotional well-being of the service user. Critics however would argue that it takes no account of structural factors/real events that seriously impede someone's social functioning. It has at best a weak evidence base, practitioners go beyond their remit for intervention, exploring areas of a person's life unrelated to the reason for intervention, and it places the practitioner in the role of 'expert' who dispenses and diagnoses.

Crisis intervention theory is interested in those in crisis and theorizes about why some people 'get over' a crisis and others do not, and become unable to function effectively and go on to repeat this behaviour at each 'crisis' or life event. Within the YJS many of the young people and their families will perceive themselves to be in crisis as a result of the offence/court appearance, but this approach, popular in generic social work, is not common in YOT work. Concepts popular to crisis theory see the event as a 'process', conditioned by the person's emotional response to the crisis and thus their ability and resilience to 'cope' rather than the given situation. Crisis theory focuses on both conscious and unconscious thought, developmental and maturational processes and is therefore influenced by psychodynamic theory. Interventions are short, time-limited, based on an emotionally supportive relationship, which assists the service user to think about coping mechanisms, alternative responses to crisis and so develop an understanding of the way they react, so that they can explore ways of adapting this for the future. It is a person-centred, immediate approach concerned with emotion and its effects on behaviour. Critics argue that social workers rarely see people in immediate crisis, that it does not recognize the reality of people's situations, nor does it take account of structural factors, that people cope differently when faced with different crisis events or in different cultures and finally, that it does not seek to explore or apportion culpability.

Task-centred work is often confused with Crisis Intervention by practitioners many of whom claim to use it. What both have in common is that they are time-limited, brief interventions aimed at dealing with a specific issue/crisis and both are often purchased as part of packages of care by employers. Task-centred is derived from a functionalist, cognitive behavioural theory base. The key elements of task-centred social work are an explicit plan in which there is an issue identified with the service user that they agree to address in a planned number of ways over a specified period of time; this includes completing given tasks between sessions with the practitioner. A key element is in the inclusion and empowerment of the service user in problem identification and the steps aimed at its solution/resolution. Critics suggest however that its power or effectiveness has been diluted through too many practitioners who misuse and misunderstand it and say they use this method when in fact they have simply undertaken a number of practical tasks. As a practitioner I found this method useful in engaging and empowering service users to learn to cope with recurring practical issues, such as calls to housing or benefits offices. In gaining the skills to do this, service users felt empowered and enabled for future life events, but supporting people effectively is time-consuming and requires considerable support to be effective. Further, task-centred work requires service users to be able to reason and act and not all service users have these faculties or are able to draw on them at the point of intervention. Critics also suggest it assumes people have the power to effect change and that it takes little account of structural factors. It is most effective with engaged participants, although 'success' at dealing with some issues can also increase and support engagement. Finally, it is argued that the time-limited nature of the engagement has 'skewed' the research findings suggesting higher levels of success because people are able to engage and sustain change over a short period. Task-centred work can be used to support other longer-term interventions however and used within a broader framework.

Intervention in the YJS

The types of intervention that exist and are available emanate from the Scaled Approach, which guides the practitioner with regard to the level and intensity of intervention into the young person's life (Chapter 7). The interventions are influenced by 'justice' and 'welfare' concepts (Chapters 1 and 4), offering practitioners the opportunity to decide whether the young person's offending requires intervention and input that aims at ameliorating housing or educational needs for example, or whether the young person's offending has no 'cause', but simply requires punishment. Research into girls and their offending patterns showed that across a range of offences girls might have different reasons to offend and that these required a variety of responses (Arnull and Eagle, 2009).

Because interventions within the YJS are decided by the 'scale' that they now 'trigger', in reality this has impacted on the ability of the professional to decide the level of intensity and type of provision. For example, the Scaled Approach gives a certain 'score' per type of offence and in so doing it gives a continual level of 'risk' to a static factor such as current/previous offence history. Thus a young person convicted of a driving offence will thereafter attract a higher score. If you remember Chapter 4 in which we discussed risk, you will recall that the actuarial basis of Asset means that it 'counts' risk based on aggregated data about risk factors; thus, with something like driving offences, which are generally committed on a prolific basis, the score will be high. The impact of this in the Scaled Approach means that for a young person who has a conviction for a driving offence that occurred by 'coincidence' in relation to the primary offence, or perhaps arising from a family argument, the professional cannot form a judgement and vary the level of 'risk' that the offence attracts – at that time or in the future. Thus although that young person may never commit another driving offence, they will always have an elevated score because of the apparent risk attached to that factor. Furthermore, the Scaled Approach may undermine the practitioner's professionalism, so that they cannot for example 'reward' success, attendance or engagement because the level and type of contact are set by the score – anecdotal evidence from practice is that this has a real and negative impact.

Some of the interventions open to practitioners are welfare-based or aimed at specific types of offending; for example, the 'knife crime prevention programme' or 'gang injunctions'; areas such as this are heavily influenced by types of offences about which government or the public become concerned and seek to react to capitals and thus may disappear or evolve over time. For example, in January 2012, County Courts were given civil powers to make gang injunctions against 14–17-year-olds with the intention of preventing gang-related violence (YJB, 2012). This helps to highlight the highly politicized nature of work in the YJS and how this influences the trajectory of interventions, as well as what is offered.

As we have seen, interventions within the YJS are heavily influenced by CBT with a focus on influencing thinking and behaviour and this applies to the groupwork programmes and some routinized forms of intervention and discussion offered on a one-to-one basis; for example, anger management or alcohol awareness. We discuss one of these programmes below, but in practice, because much work is delivered on a one-to-one basis (often by social workers) the methods of intervention used are varied, with an individual practitioner working in a way in which they were trained or choosing to interpret the package on offer. Other interventions which should be standard, but which in practice vary across YOTs, focus on specialist input and support; these are usually welfare-related (although they may have a crimino-genic value or effect) – thus housing, education, substance misuse and mental health. Whether or not the YOT has specialist workers based within it, or the level of access to specialist support in community-based teams, reflects not only the strength and acceptance of multi-professional and inter-agency working but also the level of need in that area that managers have decided is required. In some areas there may therefore be a substance use worker, but no housing officer or specialist support; such decisions may also be the subject of local political decision-making and fit the profile an area holds of itself (Chapter 3).

Interventions within the YJS can have a number of 'facets' and these require-ments can be attached to a Youth Rehabilitation Order (YRO): Supervision, Activity, Programme, Intensive Supervision and Surveillance, Intensive Fostering, Intoxicating Substance Treatment, Drug Treatment, Drug Testing, and/or Mental Health Treatment, Curfew, Unpaid Work and Attendance Centre Requirement. As you can see the options are broad; essentially what they all encompass is either some form of one-to-one work, specialist support where required, some victim work/community reparation and differing levels of intensity of contact and curtailment of freedom. All of these are decided by the assessment process and therefore relate to the levels of need and risk that are identified. A generic understanding of the theories that underpin this range of intervention opportunities is therefore essential. This allows social workers and practitioners within the YJS to understand what is being asked for and enables them to think through how they may/may not choose to engage with the interventions and proposed directions travelled. For although the exact nature of each named intervention may change over time, the underpinning core theories are the same, and this is key to understanding the nature of social work in the YJS and the challenges and dilemmas it poses.

Social workers will be heavily involved in assessing young offenders, writing Pre-Sentence Reports (PSRs) and making recommendations for intervention. We have discussed the generic social work methods that underpin interventions above and have talked about how these are also brought into play by individual practitioners in one-to-one work. The level and intensity of intervention will be varied according to the 'risk' that the young person is seen to pose and thus some young people can be seen by a practitioner/YOT three times a week, while others will be seen much less frequently. As noted much of this is determined currently via the Scaled Approach; we consider interventions, such as Intensive Surveillance and Supervision Programme (ISS) delivered to high-risk young offenders in Chapter 10. Supervising practitioners will not be responsible for delivering all of the interventions offered to a young person and will therefore need to be able to assess and plan for these interventions and then case manage their delivery (Chapter 3). However, social workers will also deliver very specific programmes as part of a planned intervention programme and as we have seen these can be complex, varied and changing. We therefore discuss below some examples of the types of intervention that are currently offered in some parts of the UK to illustrate the diversity, the differing methods on which they draw and the range of work a practitioner might be engaged in planning or delivering.

The **Knife Crime Prevention Programme** was created in response to public and political concerns about knife carrying and use in the UK which developed as the result of a number of deaths of young men, and which received high levels of media coverage in the early 2000s. These occurred principally in the south of England but the programme can be used by any YOT in the UK. It is aimed at 10–17-year-olds who have been convicted of an offence in which there is use of, or the threat of use of, a knife. It can be recommended in a PSR and the court must specify it as part of an intervention plan where it forms part of a YRO. It is one of the programmes influenced by CBT and is delivered over eight weeks in group or individual format, with a focus on behaviour and consequences, reinforced with educational elements:

- attitudes to knife carrying;
- health;
- laws surrounding knives and weapons;
- managing conflict and anger;
- peer education;
- public space awareness;
- social implications of knife possession;
- victim interaction.

There is no evidence to date of the scale of its use or its effectiveness in tackling knife crime and knife carrying. Although it can be used with any 10–17-year-old, knife carrying has to date been associated mainly with boys, with girls rarely carrying and using weapons in offences of violence (Arnull and Eagle, 2009). Anecdotal evidence suggests the programme is used, but is often shortened/adapted as practitioners consider it would not engage the young person for eight weeks.

Family and Parenting Programmes are another recently available intervention within the YJS. The programmes are aimed at improving the parenting skills and/ or engagement with the child of parents of young offenders/those at risk of offending. The programmes appear systemic as they target the broader social causes for the young person's behaviour, and are in keeping with the YJB's original remit, to also 'prevent' offending. However, as interventions, the programmes draw on behavioural theory and were created in response to theorizing, which identified social issues as arising from 'problem' families. Concerns about social exclusion have ranged across the political spectrum and have been differentially interpreted and promulgated by those from the Left and Right (Arnull, 2007), but the premise was accepted by New Labour and informed many of their social policies, ranging from Sure Start to the Respect Agenda. Similar concerns underlie the Troubled Families Agenda (2012) and it is not clear how these will intersect. In practice, parenting programmes are often controversial because they can be required of families where there has been no criminal activity, but where the family or child(ren) is assessed as anti-social and they seek to disrupt this pattern; thus they might form part of a range of interventions with a young person via a Youth Inclusion and Support Programme (YISP). The YJB argues that the core principle 'is the utilisation of a key worker who organises services and proactively engages the family using a more assertive approach to providing support'. They cite the Department for Education (2010) research as evidence of the effectiveness of parenting programmes and argues that this is in part due to the key worker who will organize a range of services and ensure engagement with the family. The key for the YJB appears to be the robust and assertive approach that it considers needs to be taken with families. However, effectiveness is by no means proven and some would argue it is predicated on the high levels of intervention, is aimed at social engineering, adopts a moralized tone and can result in carceral policies and scapegoating. In a recent study looking at women's experiences in Family Support Services, Parr (2011) found that these effects were present, but that the multidimensional focus of the projects on structural and welfare needs such as housing, education, health and benefits did result in improvements. She suggested the disciplinary effects were ameliorated by the 'non-stigmatising and sensitive' approach of many of the family workers who were also usually working-class women (Parr, 2011: 732). Her findings are congruent with other studies that we have discussed, suggesting that relationship-based work with a clear and appropriate communication style can result in effective engagement and lead to change; these aspects of intervention appear to be essential to effectiveness, but also mitigate the policy basis and method of intervention. As a practitioner this is a key message for work within the YJS.

Despite all of the possible interventions within the community some young people will be sentenced to custody, which may result in them being held in a Secure Children's Home (10–16) or a Young Offender Institution (YOI) (16–18). On a positive note, between 2006/7 and 2010/11, there was a marked decrease in the number of young people under the age of 18 sent into custody and this occurred particularly in the younger age cohort. This is good both because of the severe restriction of liberty, which should only be used where an offence is so serious as to warrant no other option, and also because custody has particularly deleterious effect on relationships, housing and work and it is accepted that levels of recidivism are high post-custody. The prison service does not appear to have been 'blamed' for these consequences in the way that the Probation Service was for the lower, but still higher than desired, levels of recidivism following community penalties; the approach taken with imprisonment appears to be that at least the person could not do any harm while in custody and therefore in itself it was inconsequential if recidivism was high. However, in recent years, there has been a focus on resettlement in the adult CJS and youth justice systems, with the Home Office publishing a strategy in 2004 leading to a refocusing in YJ entitled 'Youth Resettlement: A Framework for Action'. Both adult and youth programmes have identified 'pathways' that require focus and action and these are:

- case management and transitions;
- accommodation;
- education, training and employment;
- health;
- substance misuse;
- families;
- finance, benefits and debt.

It is suggested that these areas provide a 'blueprint for effective action' but they are the areas that resettlement work always focused on. These had been a large part of adult work in the probation service but were drastically cut in the 1990s with no provision being offered to those serving less than 12 months – which was the bulk of offenders in custody; sometimes therefore practice 'swings' between trajectories and you will observe this. Resettlement work is therefore reprioritized within the YJS as a result of the problems that were found to occur when work in this area was given lower priority. Again the suggested pathways form a more holistic attempt to engage both with other professionals and agencies on the understanding that the more effective those links are, the more effective the intervention and support will be. It is also emphasized that this offers an opportunity to link with and meet the needs of the diversity of young offenders and thus go beyond standard interventions and programmes. And given the emphasis under New Labour about 'joined-up working', there is now more recognition within the broad scope of social welfare services that there should be joint working, co-operation and interaction – where this works well it is effective and does benefit the service user. This type of language has been mirrored in the current localization policies.

National Standards

Interventions within the YJS are delivered subject to National Standards that set guidance about timelines, levels of contact, and so on in prescriptive detail. We are not going to discuss the detail of these as they govern every aspect of the process of engagement with young people in the YJS. Interventions are covered in Section 8 of the National Standards and these guidelines have been useful in establishing consistent standards across England and Wales. They offer YOTs and practitioners an opportunity to demonstrate that they work to the National Standards and thus good, hard work can be recognized. The downside is that they can also be limiting and overly prescriptive. They are the representation of the drive under New Labour to modernize and deliver good and effective services to high standards, but alongside that came a strong managerial agenda that has provoked considerable debate (Arnull, 2008; Feeley and Simon, 1996). Regular inspections of YOTs are undertaken and the reports are detailed, often focusing on specific YOTs and/or areas of work. A recent inspection in 2011 looked at the provision and delivery of offending behaviour, health and education, training and employment interventions (IYO/CJJI, 2011). It was in general positive and found that assessments were good regarding the likelihood of reoffending. However, in keeping with previous studies (Arnull et al., 2005; Arnull and Eagle, 2009), the inspectors found that the assessment was not then directly reflected in the planned interventions offered or undertaken nor in clarity about what was being targeted and what would be achieved (important in CBT work and brief interventions).

Further, in accordance with research findings (Arnull ct al., 2007) and as discussed in Chapters 4, 5 and 6, they 'found little use being made of individual and aggregated outcome data to improve services' (IYO/CJJI, 2011: 5) nor 'systematic analysis of YOT offending behaviour intervention needs' (2011: 5) or use of the national guidance (and therefore research findings too) to aid local planning and interventions. This indicates that despite a heralded move to effective evidence-based interventions, to a highly integrated and computerized system with easily aggregated data and CBT and brief interventions with clear plans, agreed targets and anticipated outcomes, YOTs have remained services whose delivery is largely based upon what exists or what they are asked to provide and not what they know and can prove is needed or works locally.

The National Standards for the YJS are currently under review and this follows the current government's agenda for more flexibility in terms of delivery of services; pilots are therefore currently being undertaken to look at the effect of varying or loosening National Standards. By varying standards the government also makes it harder to compare previous levels of performance and delivery against current achievement and in times of significant cuts this might also be to their benefit. However, at the same time the YJB is also developing and consulting on an 'assessment and planning interventions: review and redesign project' and this proposes ensuring:

- Specific outcomes to work towards for individual young person in the short, medium and long term.

- Targets/steps needed to achieve those outcomes including targets on how to make use of support networks and strengths in the young person's life and ensuring balance (where required) between constructive and restrictive measures.

- Promoting participation and engagement through identifying responsivity factors (for example, learning preferences) and addressing practical barriers.
(Teli, 2011: 24)

Clearly, these look as though they are seeking to respond to some of the issues identified by research and the 2011 Inspection Report. They are in keeping with CBT and brief interventions methods and they appear to seek to address some ethical concerns about the restrictions imposed on young people by the intensity of some interventions. They are also cognizant of more recent concerns within the YJS about the learning styles and abilities of many of the young people subject to interventions.

EXERCISE

Using the case study, on page x, think through how you might intervene. Outline your theory base and thus the method indicated. Draw up a plan of intervention, work to be undertaken, the targets to be met and how you will evidence that. Is your plan congruent with current YJS practice? If yes, how? If no, why do you consider this more appropriate?

Note

1   These are of necessity covered briefly and for a more full, although general discussion of social work methods and theories, see Wilson et al. (2008), Richards et al. (2005) and Payne (1997).

7

The Scaled Approach to sentencing disposals and supervision

LEARNING OUTCOMES

By the end of this chapter you should be able to:

*   Understand the sentencing structure and disposals used in the Youth Justice System (YJS).

*   Understand the Youth Rehabilitation Order (YRO) and utilize intervention levels.

*   Appreciate that 'spaces' can be found for creative practice within standardized youth justice responses.

The Scaled Approach established major changes in youth justice (YJ) practice and legislation in England and Wales. It implemented a tiered approach to interventions in order to reduce the likelihood of reoffending and risk of serious harm (Youth Justice Board, 2010). This approach was designed to complement the introduction of the YRO, which was initially introduced as part of the Criminal Justice Act (2003), and amended in the Criminal Justice and Immigration Act (2008). The Scaled Approach aims to prevent the likelihood of reoffending by young people by tailoring the intensity of the intervention to the assessment and more effectively managing the risk of serious harm to others (Youth Justice Board, 2010b). This order is a generic community sentence for children and young people who offend and combines the nine existing sentences (with sixteen various requirements) into one generic sentence. It is the standard community sentence (including community licence from custody) used for the majority of young offenders. It aims to simplify sentencing for young people, while improving the flexibility of intervention (Youth Justice Board, 2010b).

Young people who are first time and/or less serious offenders and who plead guilty at the first opportunity are the exceptions to the YRO criteria. If the offence is not serious enough for custody to be considered and the young person does not meet the criteria for a Hospital Order, Absolute Discharge or Fine, then the sentencing bench will impose a Referral Order of between 3 and 12 months' duration and commensurate with the level of seriousness of the offence (Youth Justice and Criminal Evidence Act 1999 amended in the Criminal Justice and Immigration Act 2008).

If however the Referral Order is not an option for the bench (if a young person appears at Crown Court, the bench must declare themselves a youth court in order to impose a Referral Order), possibly due to previous non-compliance or the young person is not eligible for this intervention due to frequency of previous offending behaviour or has entered a not guilty plea and if custody is not being considered, then the young person will be given a YRO. Therefore, the judiciary must consider that the offence is serious enough to warrant a YRO, and the restriction of liberty involved must be proportionate to the seriousness of the offence (Criminal Justice Act 2003, ss 147–48).

The YRO reflects the move towards a more individualized risk and needs-based approach to community sentencing, and is seen as enabling greater choice from a 'menu' of requirements (see Figure 7.1). A young person can be sentenced numerous times to a YRO with the requirements being adapted from the menu as appropriate to deal with the offending behaviour. However, in particular cases, for example, where the young person is already subject to a YRO Reparation Order (the Court must revoke any previous YROs as an individual can only be subject to one order at a time unless on a Detention Training Order Licence when YRO can begin at conclusion of the Licence period), the court cannot sentence to a YRO unless the existing orders have been revoked. The Court also has the power to order a sentence review in particular YRO cases (Youth Justice Board, 2010b). The court will specify the date or dates by which particular requirements must be completed; the maximum period of a YRO is three years. The Pre-Sentence Report (PSR) must make very clear what the proposed Scaled Approach intervention level will be where the author is proposing a YRO with supervision requirements.

The YOT practitioner assesses the levels of intervention required to aid the cessation of offending by the young person based on the Asset score 0–64 (see Chapter 5) and the level of risk posed by the young person is mapped against the three intervention levels: Standard, Enhanced and Intensive outlined in Table 7.1. On completion of the Asset, a score of 0–14 inclusive would indicate that the assessment identifies the young person as low risk of likelihood to reoffend and low risk of serious harm and therefore a standard level of intervention is required. Scoring 15–32 establishes the young person as medium likelihood and medium risk of reoffending and serious harm and therefore requiring an enhanced level of intervention. An intensive level of intervening by the YOT and partner agencies would be required if the score is in the range of 33–64 as this denotes the young person as being of high risk and high likelihood of serious harm and reoffending behaviour.

As you may recall the Asset score is related not just to the offence and its seriousness but also to other social, psychological, physical and mental health factors deemed to be relevant in a young person's life. The Youth Justice Board (YJB) guidance for the Scaled Approach states that interventions identified through the use of the Asset should be supported by professional judgement. In addition, the government's response to the consultation document 'Breaking the Cycle' states a renewed confidence in the expertise of 'professionals' rather than the 'unworkable sentencing framework and a statute book littered with over-prescriptive law' to address offending behaviour (Ministry of Justice, 2010). The document uses the words 'freedom' and

Table 7.1 YRO: supervision frequency matrix

Intervention level	Minimum number of contacts per month for first three months of order	Minimum number of contacts per month for remainder of order
Standard	2	1
Enhanced	4	2
Intensive	8	4

'discretion' when discussing how professionals will be able to go about the business of reducing offending, recidivism and working with future victims.

However, history shows that government rhetoric does not always manifest itself into practice. For example, the incoming Coalition Government suggested radical changes to the way young people who committed offences or were considered at risk of offending would be dealt with. However, in November 2011, they announced a u-turn to their proposals leaving the basic structure of the YJB, created by New Labour, in place.

At the time of writing, this publication on how professional judgement and discretion would manifest itself was not clear. However, the current approach, which it appears will now remain in place for the foreseeable future, establishes the Scaled Approach as very prescriptive. Once an Asset score has been ascertained, which for many of the categories does not require professional judgement, then the level and frequency of intervention are already defined through the, standard, enhanced and intensive levels of intervention scale (Sutherland, 2009). However there are a number of variable factors that may lead some young people to be scored higher or at least differently from each other, depending on who is undertaking the assessment, the YOT's resources and also on how the seriousness of crime is interpreted geographically (Chapter 1).

The frequency of supervision assessed by the practitioner must be highlighted by the author in the PSR in accordance with the minimum standards (see Table 7.1)

The YJB's guidance on the possible sentence structures by intervention outlined in Table 7.2 highlights the availability of certain options to practitioners when considering their court reports and assessments.

While acknowledging that these tables are only guidance, supervision to varying degrees along with reparation activities would be the staple response for most young people attending the YOT.

Of concern to YJ practitioners and possibly more so social workers are the notions of 'risk and 'need' that will become apparent through the Asset assessment process with a young person and could possibly have a counterproductive effect on the scoring levels. For example, the young person may be out of school through expulsion and may be homeless as well. Using the Asset you may score these two categories a high 4 perhaps as this identifies the offender as having an unstructured day and no accommodation placing them at greater risk of reoffending. Alternatively, you see the

Table 7.2 YRO: sentence structure by intervention table

Intervention level	Function	Typical case management approach	Possible sentence requirement/component (not exclusive)
Standard	Enabling compliance and repairing harm	Organizing interventions to meet basic requirements of order	Reparation
			Stand-alone unpaid work
			Supervision
		Engaging parents in interventions and/or to support young person	Stand-alone attendance centre
		Monitoring compliance	
		Enforcement	
Enhanced	Enabling compliance and repairing harm	Brokering access to external intervention	Supervision
	Enabling help/ change	Co-ordinating interventions with specialists in YOT	Reparation
			Requirement/component to help young person or change behaviour (e.g. drug treatment, offending behaviour programme)
		Providing supervision	
		Engaging parents in interventions and/or supporting young person	
		Providing motivation to encourage compliance	Combination of the above
		Proactively addressing reasons for non-compliance	
		Enforcement	
Intensive	Enabling compliance and repairing harm	Extensive	Supervision
	Enabling help/ change and ensuring control	Help/change function plus additional controls, restriction and monitoring	Reparation
			Plus
			Requirement/component to help young person or change behaviour
			Requirement/component to monitor or restrict movement (e.g prohibited activity, curfew, exclusion or electronic monitoring)
			Combination of the above

young person being more vulnerable and more of a risk to themselves than to others but still at risk of further offending and score them the same but for very different reasons. The scoring could result in quite a high level of intervention that may be unwarranted as housing issues and education would need to be addressed by partner agencies with representatives within or external to the YOT. Therefore an additional supervision meeting a week with the supervising officer will not remedy the situation. However, it does mean that the YOT case worker becomes the case manager responsible for more than just addressing the offending behaviour (Chapter 3).

To reiterate, prior to the YRO there were a number of disposals available to the court when addressing a young person's offending behaviour. These disposals were often used in a tariff system with the least intensive used at the beginning of an offender's career and increasing in frequency and intensity if they progressed through the system. The merit of this approach was that it ensured that first time less serious offenders did not receive overly punitive interventions. However, the demerit was that the procedural nature of the sentencing framework meant that serious first time offenders did not receive the levels of supervision required to address their behaviour when it would potentially have the most effect.

Therefore the emphasis of the Scaled Approach and the YRO is on practitioner assessment skills using the risk assessment tools identified in earlier chapters such as Asset and the Pre-Sentence/Referral Order Report combined with a clear understanding of the service user's personal, social and criminal history. The notions of honesty and integrity are also key to a good working relationship with young people even if there are times when you are required to take punitive action. You may need to return the young person to court as they have breached an order or not complied sufficiently. This places the worker in a difficult position, but being clear and establishing boundaries are essential in a supervisory relationship and will help to alleviate this.

An additional dilemma is that the sentencing tariffs do not explicitly allow for successful outcomes or 'changes' to influence future offending behaviour and therefore sentence disposals. For example, if we take the case where a young person's criminality over time has increased in frequency but may have reduced in seriousness, unless the YOT worker highlights this in a report or a court officer argues this in court, the judiciary may automatically hand down a harsher sentence. These notions of success may not concur with a societal view, where only complete desistance from crime is acceptable. However, YOT workers and young people need to celebrate accomplishments no matter how small as these will help increase self-esteem and confidence in young people.

Where a young person is starting to turn around their life and is taking positive steps to change their offending behaviour, if they are taken to court for sentence for an offence committed some considerable time in the past and they are punished more severely for the less serious matter that does not acknowledge their progress, this can have a very negative impact on the young offender. There are numerous factors that may influence the young person's level of offending and desistance such as getting older, finding a boyfriend or girlfriend, home life, school or employment and the YOT's interventions. The difficulty for practitioners is that it is almost impossible to know what factors or combinations of factors have a direct correlation with the positive or negative influences on offending behaviour.

However, there is acknowledgement in the literature that many young people simply grow out of crime and this correlates with maturational developmental theories and processes (Milner and O'Bryne, 2009; Smith and McAra, 2004; Flood-Page et al., 2000). Some authors identify childhood as a dual dimensional process of both structure and context (James et al., 1998). This reflects the social construction of children and childhood that encompasses age-related and culturally defined societal assumptions, along with the physical and psychological milestones of development (Llewellyn et al., 2008). YOT practitioners require a comprehensive understanding of how society creates and views youth and young offenders and this in turn needs to be linked with developmental milestones that can influence levels of capacity of the children and young people to understand their culpability and more broadly their involvement in the YJS.

A YOT practitioner will need to reflect and think critically about the young person's actions, identifying possible patterns and looking for rationales for their behaviour. The worker will draw on their theoretical knowledge and practice experience to assess and possibly intervene above and beyond the narrowly prescribed parameters of established statutory interventions as many needs do not fit neatly into tick boxes.

Summary

There are a number of issues raised by the use of the Scaled Approach and YRO that you as a class may wish to discuss further. These may include the notions of professional judgement, resources, the quality of supervisory relationships, ethical considerations, Anti-Oppressive Practice (AOP) and Anti-Discriminatory Practice (ADP).

The notion of professional judgement has numerous implications and contradictions as the YOT is made up of a number of professionals each with a varying professional training (see Chapter 3), which may affect how individuals perceive, use and score the Asset. A drug misuse worker may view and score the young person's drug use on Asset as low. However, the social worker or police officer may view this as much higher. There is some anecdotal evidence that newly qualified or less experienced workers score each category of the Asset higher than more seasoned practitioners for fear of getting the assessment wrong. One may also view professional judgement from a more cynical perspective and it could be suggested that some practitioners may score a young person's risk of reoffending and risk of harm lower than it actually is to reduce frequency and contact times with that particular youth. Workload pressures and other professional or personal issues may contribute to a worker taking a lenient view of some cases referred to them.

This 'risk-led' approach binds the practitioner and the judiciary to particular disposals. However, there is flexibility within the model to allow for more intense supervision work to be carried out with a young person who had committed a more serious first time offence than was previously available. Under the old tariff system prior to YRO many young people were given disposals based on the frequency of their offending rather than the severity. Many times during my practice I was very frustrated when meeting a young person in court who had committed a fairly serious crime who was given an order that did not require them to undertake sufficient super-vision to address their behaviour. Often the consequence would be that the young person committed more offences and only after a considerable amount of time possibly find that they were undertaking the levels of intervention required, although also possibly finding themselves bordering on a custodial sentence. The Scaled Approach sought to redress the balance giving practitioners more discretion at the assessment stage to ask the judges/magistrates for a particular order at any time during the career of a young offender with various levels of intervention suitable to address the criminogenic needs of the young person.

Some studies have identified geography as playing a part in determining how serious some offences are seen by the judiciary and practitioners especially where the prolification of more serious crime is seen as the norm (Youth Justice Board, 2004). This often manifests itself in urban and rural regional disparities where cities have a greater frequency of serious crime and therefore when working in an urban YOT you may find yourself working with more serious and prolific offenders than in a more rural location. The reasons for these differences are varied and beyond the scope of this book but are related to numerous social factors including population numbers, level and types of policing including detection and funding for YOTs and the police service.

In terms of financial implications for the YJS, the funding for YOTs is based on the pooled budgets of the multiple agencies involved in the team. These in turn are based on population numbers and therefore inner city boroughs may experience a greater intensity of offending but also are provided with additional funding and there-fore resources. More rural areas have a dispersed population, less crime and fewer resources to address anti-social behaviour (ASB). Available resources impact on the way many YOTs deliver the requirements of the disposals given, therefore, not only can the sentence differ from one location to another but the experiences of the same order may also differ considerably depending on YOT partner arrangements and financial resources (Chapter 3).

In certain geographic locations many young Black and Minority Ethnic young males are sentenced more severely (Wilson and Moore, 2004; Youth Justice Board, 2004; Goldson, 2002). This can be addressed in the reports written to the court and we consider it an ethical duty for practitioners to identify these issues in their written assessment where the sentencing of Black Minority Ethnic (BME) groups is concerned. It is understandable to a degree where workload pressures dictate that reports become standardized and certain crimes receive certain levels of supervision and specific inter-ventions. This is possibly more so where YOT resources are limited; however, the practitioner can call on their creativity and knowledge to write an ethical report that is culturally sensitive. The literature suggests that young men from Asian backgrounds respond more effectively to community sentences that address reparation directly within their own communities than with other types of sentence especially custody and more generic community restoration (Ammar, 2001). Therefore being creative and using your academic skills, a report writer could tailor their assessment to address the individual needs of the offender in a culturally sensitive and proficient way rather than following a prescribed set of standard interventions. This obviously relates to other areas of marginalization and oppression that may impact on the young person's life such as ablism, gender, religion, age and sexuality (Milner and O'Bryne, 2009).

The acknowledgement of the codes of practice and ethics and their resonance with one's own beliefs do not by any means excuse 'workers from the necessity of considering painful solutions' for service users (Clifford and Burke, 2004: 316). The balancing of ethical practice with professional duties often conflicts with notions of personal and moral belief systems, establishing a process that requires empathy and understanding more than just technical skills that can be applied to the assessment process.

While it is acknowledged that the various professionals working in YOTs do so in partnership with each other, the same is equally true for the micro partnership working with children and young people. Using the service user relationship to engage with young people is a key element in achieving aims and objectives agreed with and decided upon between the worker and service user.

YOT practitioners by the very nature of the justice system have substantial power and must therefore be aware of this power and the responsibilities that go with it. Foucault in his work on power used the term 'spaces' which in relation to social work can correlate with the areas between nebulous policy and the application of practice (Evans and Harris, 2004). It is the areas of 'uncertainty' that allow for practitioner discretion and provide the possibility for innovative and creative practice. These 'spaces' can occur in the assessment and referral processes and also the one-to-one supervision of service users where YOT workers can influence notions of risk and harm and which services that subsequently may or may not be received by the service users. Therefore practice may be constrained by the Asset and subsequent prescribed interventions. However, professional discretion can occur in places within those interventions.

Many legislative and policy decisions seek to influence practice in a particular manner, but in reality YOT interventions and protocols do not necessarily achieve what is intended (Arnull, 2011). The rhetoric versus reality debate appears common-place with the YJS and can have far-reaching effects on many young people's lives; for example, criminal records and the lack of education and employment opportunities (Zernova, 2007). Although the YRO, Asset, Pre-Sentence and Referral Order Reports are prescribed, somewhat standardized and therefore problematic if used as a baseline assessment rather than the benchmark level for intervention, there are many opportunities for creative, ethical and AO and AD practice.

EXERCISE

Using our generic case study on page x as a group or individual reflect and discuss the issues below:

- What level of risk do you think that J poses?
- What score would you give her? How does this correlate with the intervention that she may need to undertake? Is this fair?
- Do you think the interventions identified in Table 7.2 are appropriate with the various levels of intervention?

- You might want to ponder on whether or not the sentence was sufficient. Was it too short, too long, the right outcome or whether given the circumstances of the offence another option could have been considered?
- What other factors may influence J's behaviour and also your assessment of the level of intervention?

Appendix

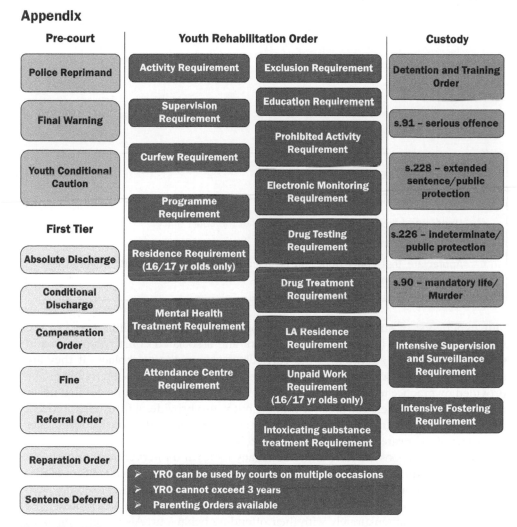

Figure 7.1 YRO: sentence options

8

Going to court

LEARNING OUTCOMES

By the end of this chapter you should be able to:

*   Understand the role and responsibilities of the court officer.

*   Understand some of the complexities of the court process.

*   Appreciate that court work can be used as an intervention with children and young people in its own right.

Our experience of studying and teaching on social work programmes and in the youth justice system (YJS) is that court work and associated court room roles and skills are given little attention in the curriculum and in the workplace. If they are addressed, it is often left to individual practice placements or on-the-job training to be provided by practice teachers, colleagues and peers. Therefore we consider that this is not only an underdeveloped area for training but it also provides a forum for students and practitioners to think and reflect critically about the role of the court, court officer and some of the related requirements of the role.

So far in this book we have addressed many issues and interventions undertaken by Youth Offending Team (YOT) social work and other professional colleagues that relate to court work without the practitioner having to attend the court setting itself. These include assessment and report writing to assist magistrates/judges sentence the young person commensurately with their offending behaviour. Also, it encompasses supervising young people on community court orders and supporting young people during sentence and on release from custodial sentences. All of these processes and interventions are post-conviction and therefore occur after the young person has attended court.

We now examine what happens after a young person has been arrested and has been detained at the police station and then subsequently appears in court. This requires us to look at the young person's initial arrest and the role of Appropriate

Adult (AA), bail (its various options including Remand and Secure Remand when bail is not granted), adjournments and court preparation. Finally, to explore sentencing and 'Breach' procedures in relation to bail or court-ordered sentences, along with using court as an intervention and general practices when servicing the courts.

In this chapter we refer to our own experiences of working in magistrate and Crown Court settings and undertaking the role of court officer in a YOT. However, we also acknowledge that locally defined practices vary from team to team and area to area. For example, as the role and responsibilities differ somewhat geographically, this impacts on the number of days that a magistrates' court will hold youth courts and this in turn reflects the population and levels of local criminality. There is a distinction made regarding youth court and adult court protocols; for example, that the youth court deals with cases where the accused is between the ages of 10 and 18. The magistrates are specially trained to deal with youth matters (as these incorporate welfare issues) and the court must sit in a court room that is not being used by the adult court. The only variation to this protocol is when a young person is charged with an offence involving an adult and therefore their case can be heard at the same time as the adult defendant in an adult court. Overall, the proceedings in youth court are intended to be less formal than those of the adult court, although to determine guilt or innocence the criminal rules of evidence and the burden and standard of proof are the same (Higher Education Academy, 2010). If a young person is charged with a very serious offence, which in the case of an adult is punishable with 14 years' imprisonment or more, the youth court can commit them for trial at the Crown Court.

The parents or carers of the young person are also summoned to court, and can be made the subject to a court order. In some cases the parent(s) of the youth can be made subject to a Parenting Order (Crime and Disorder Act 1998), which was part of the Youth Justice's Board 'Positive Parenting' agenda and was designed to make parents participate in a parenting support and education service/programme in a form directed by the court or their local YOT (Youth Justice Board, 2001). Ultimately, the rationale for the Parenting Order was to make parents more accountable and responsible for their children's behaviour. This places an onerous liability on parents and carers as 'failure to comply with the terms of the Order can result in criminal "breach" proceedings, a return to court and potentially a fine or a further Order being made' against them (Youth Justice Board, 2001: 3). The youth court is therefore very different in approach, powers and procedures from the magistrate's court sitting in its adult role, where it can only prosecute adults for offences committed by them and not their dependants.

The youth court works closely with the YOT and is guided by two considerations – the welfare of the child/young person and the prevention of offending by juveniles (Crime and Disorder Act 1998). Depending on the size of the YOT there will be either a court officer or a court team from the YOT attending court on youth court day(s). This variation reflects a locally defined court officer's role and although this may vary from YOT to YOT there are some standard responsibilities. These include being an Appropriate Adult, preparation for court, attendance and servicing the youth court and will involve the role of the court officer, court room knowledge, confidence and experience and above all establishing a good professional working relationship with key personnel at the court.

Appropriate Adult (AA)

When the young person is arrested they are taken to the police station to be questioned about their offending behaviour. The Police and Criminal Evidence Act 1984 (PACE) is the legislation that safeguards the offender's rights and ensures their physical and emotional well-being during the questioning process. One role that the social worker in the YOT may undertake is that of AA. PACE regards an AA as an impartial adult available to safeguard the rights and civil liberties of a child or young person who is detained and questioned by the police. The role is an interesting one for the YOT worker as they may become somewhat compromised as some of what they may hear in a police interview may later be needed in a court report. In addition, YOTs technically only work with convicted offenders and the role of AA is therefore a deviation from the traditional YOT role, as the young people in these cases have yet to go to court. The practitioner may actually hear more than they can write about as the young person, although possibly guilty of all matters, may only be charged with some due to lack of evidence. The YOT report can only reflect what has been admitted by the youth.

The role of AA may be extended to the court room if the parents or guardian of the youth are not in attendance when the bench wishes to pass sentence. The role as with the police interview is to again ensure that the young person understands what is going on and what the outcomes are. The court and YOT encourage family and/or other carers to attend the court where possible to avoid this potential compromise in responsibilities. Many YOTs work with external organizations who provide AAs for young people or they may have dedicated staff whose role is not to subsequently supervise the young person; this helps to avoid some of the issues raised concerning AA duties.

Court preparation

Regarding best practice, the YOT may receive a list from the court the day before youth court occurs identifying the young people attending on that day, giving name, age and the address of attendees. As the police often charge and then bail the young person to the next available youth court date, additional names may appear on the day for those young people arrested the day or night before the youth court convenes. The YOT court officers on duty should then prepare or ensure reports and subsequent documentation relating to each case is available to assist the magistrates. These fall into five categories:

1   First time attendees with no previous convictions and potential bail issues.
2   Previous known offenders appearing on new matters.
3   Previously known offenders who are being sentenced and therefore reports have been written about them.
4   Young people from other areas not known to the local YOT that may fit any of the above categories.
5   Young people already on a court order who have breached the conditions of their sentence by either missing appointments normally on the third occasion (this

number is left to practitioner discretion; however, if breach is not instigated at this point it must have manager's agreement) or by inappropriate or threatening behaviour to either staff or other young people at the YOT.

1. First time attendees with no previous convictions.

Little is required from the court officer when the attendee is in court for the first time as the YOT will not have any database records for that young person. In addition, the youth would not have pleaded to the offence they have been charged with and therefore if a 'not guilty' plea is entered then only possible bail issues will arise depending on the severity of the offence. If a 'guilty' plea is entered as stated in the previous chapter only a Referral Order is available to the sentencing bench if Custody, Hospital Order or Conditional Discharge is not a consideration (Youth Justice and Criminal Evidence Act 1999 amended Criminal Justice and Immigration Act 2008).

The other alternative that may occur in either of the first two options is that an adjournment may be asked for. In the first option this could be for the defence solicitor to view evidence not available on the day and therefore leaving their client unable to plead. In the second option (not so likely, and in my experience it only happens on rare occasions), the bench may consider the offence so serious that they are considering custody and therefore ask for a written report from the YOT to assist in their decision-making.

Bail

The Magistrates' Courts Act (1980) sets out the magistrates' powers to grant or refuse bail and the principal legislation regarding remand decisions is the Bail Act (1976). There is a general right to bail for any person in criminal proceedings. The court must always consider granting bail; however, there are exceptions to the right to bail, based on set criteria. Measures such as Bail Supervision, Bail Intensive Supervision and Surveillance and/or tagging can be used to address concerns about granting bail.

Under the Bail Act (1976) bail can be refused under the following conditions: if there are substantial grounds for believing that the young person may offend on bail, fail to return to court at the specified date and/or obstruct justice/interfere with witnesses.

In deliberating this, the court must also consider:

*   the nature and seriousness of the offence;
*   the young person's offending history (or lack of);
*   strength of community ties (family, education);
*   history of compliance with bail;
*   strength of evidence in the case.

There are some additional exceptions: for example, if the young person is already serving a sentence; for the young person's own protection or welfare; if there are previous breaches of bail conditions; or is unlikely to co-operate or attend interviews without being in custody if the case is adjourned for inquiries or a report.

There are a number of types of bail. However, the starting point for the court must be the consideration of 'Unconditional Bail'. This occurs when there are no substantial objections to bail, that is, no grounds for concluding that the young person will either offend, fail to surrender or will interfere with witnesses. If unconditional bail is deemed inadequate then 'Conditional Bail' will be considered and may incorporate: conditions such as exclusions, reporting, curfew, non-contact, and so on. Conditions should be used only for reasons of preventing offending, ensure attendance at court and to prevent interference with witnesses.

When a young person is charged for an offence by the police they are bailed from the police station to appear at the next available youth court date. However, if the youth has committed a serious offence or they are already on bail then the police have to bring the offender before the court as soon as possible to allow the magistrates to decide upon whether bail is an appropriate option in terms of the risk posed to society by the defendant. On these occasions and if the next day is not a usual youth court session then the YOT will be contacted by the court to send a staff member to assess the bail options available to the court. The court officer attends court and assesses the young person in the cells in relation to offering a comprehensive bail package to address the issues raised regarding not granting bail. The assessment will cover the areas outlined below:

- Bail Asset;
- seriousness of the offence;
- grounds for denying bail;
- review antecedents and pending matters;
- risk to public (circumstances of current and previous offences);
- current bail arrangements;
- response to previous Bail Supervision and Support.

This will entail undertaking the bail assessment tool (Asset) that will investigate the levels of risk posed to and by the young person in relation to reoffending and possible interference with witnesses and also issues such as suitability of accommodation. For example, whether the young person can return to their home address or whether alternative arrangements can be made and if electronic surveillance equipment can be installed at the house (this requires owner's consent). Close co-operation with police colleagues is then undertaken to investigate the suitability of any alternative bail addresses which are given to ensure their appropriateness and the safety of the young person.

Once the young person is brought before the bench then the court officer will present the magistrates with the bail package and could be called upon to answer questions about its suitability. Where bail is refused by the court and the young person is aged between 10 and 16, the magistrates may consider a Remand into Local Authority Accommodation (RLAA) with conditions attached as necessary. This type of bail package places a duty on the local authority to provide accommodation for the young person and may also place requirements on the local authority to secure compliance with the identified bail conditions. The court is unable to stipulate the specific placement address often due to a local authority shortfall in appropriate placement provision, therefore the young person is bailed into local authority care.

Another option under the RLAA is that the local authority can apply for a Secure Order under s. 25 Children Act (1989), and Secure Accommodation Regulations (1991) and (1992). The criteria for this order is that the young person is under 14 years of age and has been charged/convicted of a violent/sexual offence or has a recent history of absconding while under RLAA conditions, and/or has been charged with an imprisonable offence while they were remanded. Also other custodial settings may be inappropriate if the young person meets a vulnerability threshold and therefore the order seeks to find accommodation other than for the purpose of restricting liberty because the young offender is likely to abscond from such other accommodation or is likely to injure themself or others if kept in such accommodation.

These heightened levels of bail restrictions reflect that there will be times when a suitable conditional bail package is not available due to the level of risk presented by the youth and therefore custody is required. This is where the court officer needs to be robustly honest with the young person and the bench about the realities of the situation. This is a difficult position especially for social work practitioners as bail assessments often mean that you are responsible for possibly depriving a young person of their liberty; however, your role is also to provide a level of safety for society. These decisions may weigh heavily on the worker's conscience; nevertheless, no matter how difficult they are, practitioners need to be self-aware and check their own moral and ethical standpoint while pursuing a decision based on an objective professional assessment.

2.   Previous known offenders on new charges.

If the young person is known to the YOT and is appearing for the first time in relation to new offences and has pleaded guilty, in some areas it has been agreed with the court that a previous report (either a Pre-Sentence or Referral Order) that is not more than six months old can be provided to assist in sentencing the matter on the day. Normally, a three-week adjournment is given to allow the YOT to complete the report and therefore the rationale is to deal with the matters in the most expedient way. In one YOT it was seen as good practice to not only provide a recent report but also an addendum written by the supervising officer informing the bench of the young person's progress since working with the YOT. Where the relationship between the supervising officer and young person was positive and also where the YOT had a good working relationship with the courts, this proved to be a very productive way of dealing with new offences for the court, reducing the number of appearances for the young person and therefore not impinging so onerously on their schooling and also reducing the workload for the supervising officer who did not have to undertake a new report.

3.   Previously known offenders who are being sentenced and therefore reports have been written about them.

When a young offender has pleaded guilty and the magistrates have asked for a Pre-Sentence Report (PSR) to be written then the case will be adjourned for a maximum of three weeks. This allows the YOT to gather background data and to interview the young person (in the presence of a significant carer where possible) to assess the risk of harm and reoffending and to advise the bench of sentencing and intervention options. On these occasions the court officer needs to ensure that the person designated to write the report (which again varies depending on YOT structure) has completed the assessment. The report should where possible have been gate-kept by colleagues or line managers for quality assurance and accuracy purposes and additional copies printed and signed by the author along with a copy of the current Asset. These documents are distributed on the court day to court clerks, magistrates/judges, Crown Prosecution Service (CPS) and defence lawyers as well as the young person, their carers and a copy for the court officer. Although the magistrates read the PSR and then sentence the offender, they are not bound by the recommendations of the author and on occasions they may decide on a completely different disposal from the one suggested by the YOT worker. If a community sentence has been passed, the court officer meets with the young person outside the court room to give written confirmation and also explain verbally the sentence and its requirements. Good practice would encompass the young person being given an appointment card with the supervising officer's name, contact details and the first meeting time directly after their court appearance.

If the young offender is given a custodial sentence then the court officer is required to see the young person in the cells and complete a Post-Court Report (PCR) to ensure that the young person understood the sentence given and to also assess levels of risk posed by the young person in relation to potential bullying or self-harm or issues of vulnerability. The court officer would also need to phone the Youth Justice Board's (YJB's) placement department that allocates prison places around the country to young people. Issues of vulnerability and risk identified by the young person to themselves or others should be notified to the placement department.

The court officer informs the young person of the prison that they are going to and also ensures that the PCR is given to the custody officers travelling with the young person and so this accompanies them to the custodial setting. It is good practice for the court officer to inform the young person's supervising officer at the YOT and the parents or carers if they are not in court of the prison location. The Asset and new Placement Information Form (PIF) are sent to the YJB via a secure email; the PCR is also faxed to the YJB as well as a paper copy going to the young person.

4.   Young people from other areas not known to the local YOT that may fit any of the above categories.

If the young person appearing at court is from another area then the above three scenarios apply with the added complication of not having any database knowledge of the offender, if they have previous convictions or if they are being sentenced. A signed PSR should be faxed or emailed from the young person's home area YOT to the sentencing YOT the day before the court appearance. It is also good practice for the court officer to contact the other YOT to speak to either the report writer if sentencing is taking place or the supervising officer if the offender is already known to the team to establish their current situation and history. In our experience this is not always the case: it may be difficult to contact the other YOT, speak to colleagues and some reports are late or of a poor quality.

In cases of poor professional practice, to avoid the young person being discriminated against and the YOT's practice and ultimately your own credibility being tarnished with the court, you will need to contact the report author. This will assist in clarifying aspects of the report and possibly gathering more information about the young person's circumstances. This will help when questions are asked about the report and also what provision has been put in place regarding the young offender's suggested sentence disposal.

5.   Young people already on a court order who have breached (as defined by National Standards) the conditions of their sentence by either missing appointments or by inappropriate or threatening behaviour to either staff or other young people at the YOT (Youth Justice Board, 2010a).

Breach

Coulshed (1991: 2) states that:

> while it is true that people do not come to us looking for a relationship, and while it is no substitute for practical support, nevertheless we are one of the few groups who recognize the value of relating to others in a way which recognizes their experience as fundamental to understanding and action.

This can be seen prominently in relation to 'breach' matters when the young person has deliberately missed appointments, failed to engage with their supervising officer or been physically or verbally abusive towards members of staff or other young people at the YOT (Youth Justice Board, 2010a). It is good practice for the YOT to have a 'breach' pack that lists all the documentation required to take a non-compliant young person back to court. However, this is not always the case and newly qualified or new members to the team can initially flounder if they are not properly inducted. Most localities will have a different set of breach papers that need to be completed and handed in at the earliest opportunity to a court clerk who will then issue a summons that is sent to the young person to appear at the earliest possible youth court sitting. In breaches of bail there is a different set of documentation to complete called the MG11 and this is usually a police statement that is completed by the YOT officer and then faxed or hand-delivered to the police station. Police officers are alerted to the breach of bail and visit the young person's home address to arrest them or, if they see the young person on the street, to bring them before the court to explain why they have missed their appointments or have not kept to the bail conditions.

The breach paperwork for both the court and the police identifies the appointment dates or activities that the young offender has missed and although only two dates are required on the documents, the reality is often that the young person would have missed many more especially once they are aware that they are going to be breached. In breach of bail cases the court officer may have to give details of the package originally offered and the reasons for non-compliance. The options available to the court are to reissue bail with the same, enhanced or decreased conditions or the young person may be remanded into custody. For example, on occasions the young person may not have complied because the initial conditions were not workable. In these cases the young person needs to return to court to have the conditions changed.

Where there has been a breach of sentence it is good practice for the young offender's supervising officer to write a breach report for the court outlining the details of the breach, why the reasons (if any) given are not acceptable and what the author believes should happen as a result of the breach. The process of breaching a young person is not necessarily negative and can be used as a positive reinforcement of boundaries with a therapeutic quality. The YJB states that:

> breach can be a positive tool to make clear to young people that the programme will be robustly enforced. If a scheme is using 'therapeutic breach' in this way, they should make clear to the court that they want to see the young person returned to the programme and make the case for why this should be done (citing other attendance, behaviour and engagement wherever possible).
>
> (Youth Justice Board, 2009)

There are some legal issues regarding breach matters that require clarification. The breach has to be admitted by the young person in court and only after they admit the breach (plead guilty) can any of the above positive interventions come into play. The relationship between young person and supervising officer is once again essential; a good positive relationship is one in which the young person is aware of the consequences of non-compliance and understands that they need to take responsibility for their actions. The breach in this case would be seen to be reinforcing firm boundaries between the worker and offender with both parties still engaging with each other while the breach process is taking place. The young person continues to comply with their court order and the YOT worker and offender continue to communicate about the possible outcomes of the breach process. The young person admits the breach; the practitioner would identify the reason for breach and outline that the youth has complied sufficiently and then suggest what they think should happen next. Where the relationship has broken down or was never fully established, the young person may resist engaging with the YOT during breach procedures. They may deny the breach, which results in a trial being arranged and one in which the court officer becomes the prosecutor on behalf of the YOT. The officer will be asked under oath to give evidence and may be cross-examined by the young person's solicitor. At times the local authority will appoint legal counsel for the YOT depending on the seriousness of the case.

During the court processes the potential for discriminatory and oppressive practice is obvious and the practitioner should use their communication skills to build a relationship quickly if they are to be of assistance to the young people and their families (see Chapter 5). Honesty and integrity, both key social work principles, are paramount in these cases. Initially engaging with youth; speaking with their legal advocates and parents, giving information and advice will help in building a positive relationship. If the young person is known to the YOT (or from another locality) and the court process is not a new one for them, you should ensure you know their history and if there is a report being used for sentencing also discuss with them the sentence suggested. The practitioner needs to be honest and realistic about sentence outcomes and allow the youth to take responsibility and be accountable for their actions rather than try to diminish the severity and precariousness of their situation, especially where custody is a consideration. It is a balancing act between remaining positive in a situation that can be depressing and negative for the young person, while being pragmatic about the outcomes of their case (see Chapter 5).

On occasions the YOT court officer may find a duality in their role especially in their relationship with the CPS and the defending legal counsels. Where the YOT practitioner or court officer has written a report/assessment in relation to bail issues or a sentence disposal, the outcomes can conflict with either the view of the CPS or the defendant's lawyer whose role is to secure the most appropriate outcome for their client. The court officer should be able to rely on their assessment skills and professional judgement, which may be challenged by either set of legal advocates. This is a rare event as the CPS and defence solicitors often agree with YOT reports, given that youth court is viewed as a specialist area of court work and YOT practitioners are seen as 'expert' in this field.

Attendance and servicing the court

The relationship between the YOT, its staff and that of the court personnel is a vital one if the interventions and processing of young people through the YJS is to be timely, efficient and commensurate. This relationship is concerned with the servicing of the court, not only on youth court days or when bail packages are required but also when legal matters require clarifying or advice is sought. During our practice the court staff were always appreciative of a timely response.

Court clerks play a pivotal role in the youth court and therefore it is good practice to befriend and build a good working relationship with them. On non youth court days they can assist in dealing with youth matters quickly allowing you to manage your work day more effectively. During bail or sentence hearings the court clerks may indicate to you what the potential outcome may be and therefore you can prepare to challenge or facilitate this in the most expedient way possible.

When new legislation is being enacted there may be the opportunity to undertake training with magistrates and clerks to assist them in understanding how the new legislation will look in terms of practice interventions with young people. This is a good way to meet with court colleagues in a less formal setting and it also allows for the opportunity to build credibility and perhaps influence how the court interprets new legislation.

Custody staff have the duty of ensuring that young people who are persistent or serious offenders are kept safe and secure in the cells prior to their appearance before the bench and either subsequently released or remanded/sentenced to a custodial setting. A good relationship with these colleagues can assist in getting information about young people in the cells before the clerks inform the YOT. They may also be able to assist with finding out where the young person is going to be placed if remanded or sentenced and provide valuable information regarding how the young person is coping in the cells and whether they are vulnerable to themselves or a threat to others. Custody officers are knowledgeable about the documentation required to accompany the young person to prison and this can be very beneficial.

Appearance

Dress codes can be a contentious issue as some argue that the power dynamics between worker and service user can be exacerbated if the practitioner wears more formal clothing. Others argue that workers should wear clothing that reflects their professional status and conveys respect (Seymour and Seymour, 2007). There are dress codes, procedures and specific protocols that are unique to the court room and although the youth court is deemed less formal than the adult court, this does not apply to the professionals involved. Although there is very little written about what YOT practitioners should wear, the expectation is that a male will wear a suit or similar and female colleagues the equivalent. There is no denying that the courts and legal system are powerful structures and processes that define a particular social situation and define its meanings (Goffman, 1959). These are especially apparent in the court room itself which has designated areas for the different professionals and their relative importance; it includes the props of clothing (judges' robes, gavel, gowns and suits) and the formal process of addressing the various parties including the victim and offender (Keating, 2002). In our opinion the role of court officer is that of adviser to the court in terms of legal matters and sentencing and also that of advocate for the young person to mediate the formal processes of the judiciary with those of working with young people and families ensuring they are aware and understand the processes.

You should attend court in good time and be ready to begin once the court is in session. You will need to identify which court rooms are designated as youth courts for the day. It is always a good policy (and manners) to introduce yourself to the usher and clerk and ensure that the documentation gathered at the YOT pre-court meeting is given to the relevant parties. The usher can assist with the court listing in terms of which young person is in which court and the order that they are likely to be seen. You are required to visit any young people in the court cells to check on their well-being and also check and greet the young people and their parents/carers who are in the waiting area.

You will have a designated seating area in the court room so that the bench knows members of the YOT are present. When the magistrates or judges enter the court room protocol dictates that all other parties stand and wait for them to sit before they do. If you leave or when you enter the court room and the bench are sitting you are again required by protocol to bow to the bench just before exiting or as soon as you enter. This exercise in protocol (which is more pronounced in the Crown Court) highlights the solemn and very formal nature of the justice system and reflects a very powerful environment.

Servicing the court

Most YOTs will have more than one court officer who attends youth court each week and the role is one of data collector, assessor, adviser and at times advocate. Results have to be carefully recorded and entered on to the YOT database and this may be manually or electronically. Trying to balance all of these roles can be quite fraught and you will need to prioritize your workload. Once you have mastered this skill then the resulting good multidisciplinary working relationships can prove invaluable, as the court clerks and ushers can prove to be very useful allies.

At times the YOT court officer may be called upon to clarify elements of a report or advise the bench on sentencing options. This may include contacting the report author to clarify details in the report or regarding the sentencing disposal. You may also be required to interview young people so that a verbal version of the PSR called a Stand Down Report or where magistrates have decided upon a particular disposal a Specific Sentence Report (a brief written report) can be utilized. The Stand Down Report works on the same principles as the addendum to the PSR that is less than six months old (mentioned above) and is only suitable for youths known to the local YOT. It can be an effective method of dealing with issues in a timely fashion. Where you are unable to gather the relevant information for a verbal report or where the offence is sufficiently serious, magistrates will adjourn the case for a more comprehensive assessment.

Court work as intervention

There are many variables that a court officer has little control over and the young person even less so, when they attend a youth court session. The offence, the report writer, the court officer, the court clerk, the magistrate or judge, the solemn surroundings and the legal advocates for the Crown and the defence all have to varying degrees the potential to influence the outcome of the young person's court appearance. It is these variables that can assist an experienced, knowledgeable and confident court officer to use the court and its process as an intervention in and of itself with the young person.

If practice interventions are gauged and increase with the severity of offending behaviour then court intervention can be seen as an opportunity to influence a young person's future actions.

Many authors have written about the use of the justice system as a mode of social control and the exercise of power by the state and its designates, that is, social workers. Theories on the use and misuse of power by social workers and related professions have highlighted the potential for it to be wielded to the disadvantage and oppression of certain client groups (Wilding, 1982; Lipsky, 1983; Wilding and Wardhaugh, 1993). However, as we have discussed throughout this book the exercise of power cannot be separated from its associated responsibilities and when used in an ethically positive and influential way can result in truly effective social work practice. In court this means making a potentially disempowering experience an intelligible one with a clear and trustworthy advocate in place to assist and advise the young person, their family and the court.

Summary and conclusion

This chapter highlights the diversity and complexity of court work and the potential for court officers to shape court outcomes for the YOT and for young people.

Although most courts, youth courts and YOTs work slightly differently, there are some general rules that can be applied; if not to the organizations of the YJS then certainly to the role of court officer. Good time management, confidence, being child-focused, having a comprehensive knowledge of YJ and child welfare legislation, the ability to conduct yourself professionally, using strong communication skills and a sound ethical and value practice base are some of the requirements of being a competent YOT court officer. The ability to work with uncertainty and having the personal and professional attributes (the use of self) that allow for honest and realistic interaction with service users when they are potentially at their most vulnerable are prerequisites for this role.

EXERCISES

1   There is very often a shortage of secure estate placements generally and finding one that meets the needs of higher-risk young people is often very difficult.

   Using our generic case study of J, a 14-year-old young woman (see p. x), discuss (in small groups) what you might do in a situation where you have identified J as vulnerable and at high risk of self-harm but the only placement allocation is that on the general wing of the secure estate which does not have the facilities to address your concerns.

   It might be useful to have a copy of the British Association of Social Work (BASW) code of ethics and the Health and Care Professions Council (HCPC) Standards of Practice to hand to possibly assist in your decision-making.

2   Fold a piece of paper in half. On one side list the attributes that you think a court officer should possess. Turn the paper over and on the other side imagine that you are a young person in court. What are the characteristics and skills that you would like to see in a YOT worker?

9

Restorative justice interventions

LEARNING OUTCOMES

By the end of this chapter you should be able to:

- Understand restorative justice philosophy, theory and practice more comprehensively.
- Identify a broad range of restorative interventions.
- Reflect on how restorative approaches can be used to address youth justice (YJ) concerns.

Restorative Justice has become synonymous with the work of the criminal and youth justice professions in the UK and many western countries. This approach has gained significant prominence in recent years with a variety of interventions being implemented across the adult and youth justice systems (YJSs).

The current Coalition Government and its predecessor have both acknowledged the use of Restorative Justice (RJ) as providing an effective and successful method in addressing offending behaviour. Until the Coalition u-turn in 2011 the Government was seeking to substantially overhaul the justice system including the YJS, and RJ was to play a major role in achieving its aims. Although the extent of the Government's changes has been reduced, the intention is still to establish effective sentencing policies that utilize the full range of RJ proposal measures (Ministry of Justice, 2010, 2011).

This strategy to enhance the use of best practice RJ approaches at all stages in the justice process with both youth and adult offenders is reinforced by recent academic and research data. Shapland et al. (2011) drew on longitudinal data from three large RJ projects to provide a very comprehensive account of the successes of particular RJ interventions (mediation and RJ conferences) for both victims and offenders.

Although not specifically legislated for within British statute, RJ has found its way into the everyday policy and practice of Youth Offending Teams (YOTs) across the country. Within this system RJ interventions encompass various family group conferencing models, mediation, reparation (including apology letter writing) and victim awareness (Mirsky, 2003; Wilcox and Hoyle, 2004).

The Crime and Disorder Act (1998), the Home Office publication *Restorative Justice: The Government's Strategy* (2003), restorative justice practices, approaches and processes and National Standards for Restorative Justice, all underpin the notion of taking responsibility for one's actions and their subsequent consequences (Home Office, 2003; Youth Justice Board, 2010a). All of the sentencing disposals across the various stages within the Crime and Disorder Act (1998) and YJ processes allow for the opportunity for RJ interventions to occur (Home Office, 2003; Dignan, 2003). For example, the Referral Order is a mainstream sentencing option based on RJ practices and the primary focus of YOT's statutory obligations in relation to RJ (Crawford and Newburn, 2003).

Restorative justice

RJ is a notoriously difficult concept to describe. However, a commonly quoted definition describes it as 'a process whereby all the parties with a stake in a particular offence come together to resolve collectively how to deal with the aftermath of the offence and its implications for the future' (Marshall, 1996: 37).

At its most efficient and effective, RJ resolves conflict and repairs harm through encouraging accountability from offenders and acknowledgement of the impact of their actions on others; it subsequently affords them an opportunity to make reparation for their behaviour. Ultimately, RJ is a problem-solving approach seeking to bring together and incorporate the views of all individuals or groups that have an interest in or have been affected by the incident (Sullivan and Tift, 2001; Thurman-Eyer and Mirsky, 2009).

RJ changes the conventional notions of crime being committed against the state, to those that focus on the victim and community where it occurred (Morris, 2002). It is valued as a way of hearing the voices of all those involved in the incident and consequently has the potential to heal and restore community relationships. This is in contrast to the established adversarial Common Law criminal justice system (CJS) in which the victim, offender and community are often silenced by the representatives of the state such as the Crown Prosecutor and defence advocates. Using RJ approaches the victim can talk about the incident in a safer forum and can ask the perpetrators to undertake certain tasks by way of their punishment and reparation.

The history of RJ is a long and extensive one. Its historical practices are rooted in both aboriginal and non-aboriginal societies, in Europe before the Norman Conquest (Van Ness, 1986; Graef, 2000) and in numerous aboriginal communities (Llewellyn and Hoebel, 1941). The latest resurgence of RJ started about 40 years ago and is thought to be embedded in the social, feminist and prisoner's rights movements of the 1970s (see Daly and Immarigeon, 1998; Liebman, 2007; Shapland et al., 2011).[1] An international perspective of the popularity of RJ highlights restorative interventions being used in North America and among many European and western societies (Umbreit and Coates, 1999) to the point where, in 2002, the United Nations Commission on Criminal Justice and Crime Prevention passed a resolution that outlined the basic principles for RJ (United Nations, 2002). Numerous countries signed up to the resolution highlighting a global commitment to RJ and its processes.

RJ interventions possess a fundamental objective: the restoring of balance, making right a wrong and repairing the social bonds that have been broken (Daly and Immarigeon, 1998). Restorative practices are underpinned by a set of values which include: Empowerment, Honesty, Respect, Engagement, Voluntarism, Healing, Restoration, Personal Accountability, Inclusiveness, Collaboration and Problem-solving (Restorative Justice Consortium, 2011).

This approach is seen by many as an umbrella term for the multiple interventions that were initially based on traditional First Nation and many faith community's values and practices (Crawford and Newburn, 2003; Dhami and Joy, 2007). These interventions intersect across welfare and justice issues and encompass familial, community and institutional based (including custodial) interventions (Dhami et al., 2009).

Models of RJ

Liebman (2007) identifies models of RJ that encompass a range of mediation approaches, including Victim Offender Reconciliation Programmes (VORPs) and Victim Offender Mediation (VOM), family group and restorative justice conferences and circles.

Wilcox and Hoyle (2004) adapted McCold and Wachtel's (2004) typology that defines the most restorative approach to RJ in terms of meeting the needs of those involved in the event (see Table 9.1).

The typology establishes a continuum regarding the degree to which an intervention is restorative. Certain practice models are seen as more restorative than others, with family group conferencing as 'fully restorative', VOM as 'mostly restorative' and financial compensation for victims as 'partly restorative'. The level of restoration is measured by how much the intervention meets the needs of those attending. Participants are defined as either primary or secondary 'stakeholders' and comprise victim and offender, their families and friends in the former category, with the addition of community, in the latter (McCold and Wachtel, 2004: 3).

As the acceptance of RJ has become more commonplace, its traditional approaches such as VORP and VOM, which mainly focus on mediated processes,

Table 9.1 RJ model typology

Fully restorative	Mostly–restorative	Partly restorative
Family group conference	Victim–offender mediation	Compensation
Community conferencing	Victim support circles	Victim services
Peace circles	Victimless conferences	Offender family services
Restorative conferences	Therapeutic communities	Family-centred social work
	Direct reparation to victim	Compensation
		Victim awareness
		Community reparation

have been extended to incorporate various additional types of restitution and reparation including community service, letters of apology and fines (Home Office, 2003). In relation to the typology model these two interventions can be seen respectively as 'mostly' and 'partly' restorative regarding the level of stakeholder participation in the process.

Additionally, the conferencing models and peace circles are seen as the optimum modes of delivering RJ. These approaches would be termed as 'fully' restorative as they seek to varying degrees to ensure a wide range of stakeholder participation (McCold and Wachtel, 2004; Shapland et al., 2011). These approaches are utilized as effective stand-alone interventions deployed in various ways throughout the child welfare and justice systems. The RJ philosophy that reinforces these approaches also underpins the Referral Order panel process. The panels are composed of local volunteers (trained by YOT) and one YOT member who create a contract of activities to restore the damage (both physical and emotional) caused by the young offender. Panel member training encompasses a wide variety of issues that community members need to be aware of, such as legislation and legal processes relating to the Referral Order and RJ training. Currently, these panels are only associated with the Referral Order sentence but the Government is looking to extend their role in the YJS.

Research on Referral Orders shows general support among magistrates, clerks/ legal advisers, panel members and YOT practitioners for this sentence. Specifically, 'Fifty-two percent of the young people surveyed found that taking part in the Panel meeting was either good or very good' (YJB, 2003: 13).

All RJ interventions vary in terms of the facilitator's role and the number and type of participants (Sharpe, 1998). Regarding conferencing models, these approaches generally rely on four main components: (1) referral; (2) preparation and planning; (3) the meeting; and (4) follow-up planning and events (Merkel-Holguin, 1996). There is a direct correlation between the effectiveness and success of RJ interventions and the extent of the preparatory work undertaken – the victim, community members, families and offender are all prepared prior to a conference to ensure their willingness to participate – along with the perpetrator's motivation to comply with the conference process and outcomes.

RJ conferencing uses a model of family group conference (FGC) that is scripted and compliance with the script used by the facilitator is often seen as the most important factor. This approach is underpinned by brief solution therapy, as it focuses on the issue or difficulty and identifies the individual's strengths to address the problem (Community Justice Forum, 1998; Dallos and Draper, 2000; De Shazer, 2003; Restorative Justice Oak Bay, 2003).

The features of this model are the emphasis on structure and formality; for example, the use of a formal script to direct and facilitate the conference process and a formalized seating plan. The model was designed specifically for use with young offenders and was adopted as a community policing technique in New South Wales, Australia in the early 1990s (O'Connell, 1998; O'Connell et al., 1999).

The other model of conferencing is the family group conference that is viewed as 'a mechanism that enables the formal state systems to work in partnership with informal family and community systems, recognising the knowledge and expertise of family and informal systems and recognising the knowledge and expertise of professional systems'

(Family Rights Group, 2003: 1).This model with slight variations was implemented to address welfare andYJ matters initially in New Zealand. However, it was subsequently utilized successfully across both systems in the UK (Mutter et al., 2008).

Research on conferencing has been undertaken globally encompassing both positivist and constructionist paradigms using numerous data collection methods (Sundell and Vinnerljung, 2004; Berzin et al., 2008; Mutter et al., 2008; Fox, 2008). Negative claims have been made in relation to the RJ conference potential for net widening, the erosion of legal rights and assumptions of community cohesion (and therefore restoration of victim and community is always possible). It does not necessarily reduce offending rates, does not address institutional racism, and can potentially re-victimize the victim (Umbreit and Coates, 1999; Roach, 2000; Morris, 2002; Fox et al., 2006).

By contrast, research data specifically from the UK relating to welfare-focused FGC highlights successful family engagement and the production of agency-agreed plans, high levels of satisfaction by attendees, cultural sensitivity and the empowerment of young people (Lupton and Stevens, 1997, 2003; Simmonds et al., 1998; Smith and Hennessy, 1998; Merkel-Holguin et al., 2003). Equally, crime data suggests that compliance rates with the conference contract were high; there were good satisfaction rates among victims and offenders and a reduction in recidivism and the fear of crime (Latimer et al., 2001; Miers, 2001; Hoyle et al., 2002; Mutter et al., 2008).

Theoretical frameworks

RJ theory locates itself within the broad spectrum of sociological crime theories, which places the causes of criminal behaviour within society and its structures, rather than within the individual (Mantle et al., 2005). The appeal of this approach reflects the notion that RJ 'emphasises the repair of harms and of ruptured social bonds resulting from crime; it focuses on the relationships between crime victims, offenders and society' (Daly and Immarigeon, 1998: 22). Shaming and reintegration are core aspects of RJ theory as the offender's relationship and connections to the victim and other community member's assist in holding them accountable and responsible for their unacceptable behaviour (Braithwaite, 1998). Subsequently, this aids decision-making and plans to support both victims and perpetrators that in turn empowers the victims and promote safety and healing (Restorative Justice Consortium, 2011).

Numerous sociological and individual theories associated with social work interventions such as empowerment, advocacy, Anti-Discriminatory Practice (ADP) and Anti-Oppressive Practice (AOP) group work, cognitive behavioural therapy (CBT), family therapy and community development can be seen in varying degrees underpinning RJ intervention, practices and processes (Preston-Shoot and Agass, 1990; Brown, 1997; Ronen, 1997; O'Neill and Heaney, 2000; Ife, 2002; Berg and Steiner, 2003; De Shazer, 2003; Mullaly, 2007). Mediated RJ processes facilitate dialogue between parties that 'utilizes the normative effect of group process to regulate behaviour – the facilitator setting the group focus serves the purpose of mediation's ground rules and is thought to be more respectful of participants' (McCold, 1999: 3). Structurally, these specific RJ approaches emphasize the devolvement of power away from the organizational and professional 'expert' to one that seeks to share power and control with all parties. This complements and interlinks with ADP and AOP, as empowerment and advocacy seek to address the abuse of structural power that affect people's lives at the macro and micro levels of society (Burke and Harrison, 2002).

Community

Community involvement is another key element in the conferencing process as the main goal is the reintegration of the young person back into their community (Zehr, 1990; Zehr and Mika, 1998). Conferencing is both a process and a location where professionals and the community can come together and work for the goal of stronger community and providing space for the perpetrator to recognize the harm they have caused. Pranis (2000) suggests that conferencing has the potential to strengthen communities, but that needs to be consciously built towards.

However, definitions and notions of community are nebulous and difficult to attain and often disguise both positive and negative propositions. Community development theory maintains that community members when mobilized can work together to achieve goals and aspirations that benefit their community. This is especially effective when people feel that through their collective actions they have a say, have more control and feel empowered to influence events and decisions affecting them and their environments (Ife, 2002).

The community when involved in problem-solving can assist in creative outcomes concerning the incident and is deemed a more productive response when facilitated by the family and community and not just professionals. Mirsky (2003: 1) believes that 'when families are empowered to fix their own problems, the very process of empowerment facilitates healing'. The wrongdoer benefits from having their family included in the proceedings and in creating a programme that directly affects them, with the hope that by providing family guidance and involvement, the family and community will take on more responsibility for their family and community lives. Community involvement helps the community to meet its own needs. This is especially important as it is not often that there is any 'recognition of the community as victim in any meaningful way' (Sarnoff, 2001: 17).

Conversely, community can sometimes seem as though it is the solution to all problems. However, Bazemore (1999: 101) points out that:

> most advocates of restorative justice recognise that there is nothing magical about community and that identifying and mobilising citizens to allow for a greater community role in rehabilitation, sanctioning, safety, and peacemaking process more reliant on non-experts will change but not eliminate the role of experts.

The community where RJ interventions are undertaken is an important consideration that acknowledges the positive role that families, extended families and community members can play in addressing many social problems. However, success will be inextricably linked to whether the community has sufficient capacity within it to address these concerns. Therefore, the potential to build 'bonding' social capital (ties with people in similar circumstances, family or neighbours) as well are 'bridging' social capital (weaker social ties: acquaintances, fellow workers, etc.) enables the opportunity to build on community capacity and create stronger communities.

Although conferencing holds great potential for creating stronger and more committed communities, safeguards do need to be put into place. It would not be viable to put in place a process that would continue to disempower those involved; therefore, it is important that conferencing models and the subsequent processes have important precautions attached to them.

Summary and critique

RJ interventions can appear at first glance a very seductive notion with its underpinning principles of service user empowerment, partnership and collaboration, power sharing and family- and child-centred approaches to decision-making (Pitts, 1990; Family Rights Group, 2003; Mirsky, 2003; Payne, 2005). It seeks to attain rehabilitation instead of retribution, restoration rather than punishment and to re-establish the community and societal bonds of collective communitarian accountability and responsibility (Daly and Immarigeon, 1998; Sullivan and Tift, 2001; Thurman-Eyer and Mirsky, 2009).

The communitarian ideals of RJ correspond very comfortably with the Coalition Government's notions of 'big society' where volunteers and local community groups become involved in the justice process. The Government's consultation paper initially identified the extended use of Referral Order Panels that are deemed a particularly restorative approach in addressing first time and less serious offending behaviour. There are also ideas of using RJ approaches pre- and post-sentence, for example, of Neighbourhood Justice Panels where local volunteers and criminal justice professionals are brought together to decide what action should be taken to deal with some types of low-level crime and disorder (Ministry of Justice, 2011).

Despite its successes RJ does have its critics. There are concerns regarding its potential for net widening and the erosion of legal rights, coercion, failing to restore victim and community, does not reduce offending rates, allows for institutional racism and re-victimizes the victim (Umbreit and Zehr, 1996; Umbreit and Coates, 1999; Young and Goold, 1999; Delgrado, 2000; Roach, 2000; Blagg, 2001; Daly, 2001; Latimer et al., 2001; Johnstone, 2002; Morris, 2002). RJ has been further questioned regarding whether discrepancies exists between the stated aims of an RJ organization and what staff say happens in practice and whether RJ practice is reflected by its underlying theory (Gavrielides, 2003; Lemonne, 2003; Shapland et al., 2004).

Research relating specifically to the Referral Order process has highlighted some discrepancies in perceived use and effectiveness. Issues of lack of victim engagement, community panel representation and problematic paternalistic decision-making along with domineering and coercive behaviour within the process have been raised (Zernova, 2007; Stahlkopf, 2009). These issues have been acknowledged to some degree in the literature, with some advocates accepting coercion as a necessary part of the system and deem the ends as justifying the means (Crawford and Newburn, 2003). Other proponents argue that 'process' is as important as 'outcomes' and therefore the core notions of empowerment, voluntary participation, honesty and respect are essential in meeting the aims of RJ (Harris, 1998).

In addition, practical issues such as the lack of training and, importantly, time to prepare for RJ interventions, will undermine the process integrity and its subsequent effectiveness. One of the major concerns for YOTs is the emphasis currently placed on providing a broad range of RJ interventions within stringent new budgetary constraints and without the time to develop the service in a manner that will make it successful and sustain longevity.

However, proponents of RJ continue to extol its virtues and identify it as an approach that 'in the UK is fast becoming the most over-evaluated and under-practiced area of criminal justice' (Hoyle, 2008). In relation to its deployment and underuse others have stated that 'We can no longer afford for Restorative Justice to be the most researched, most effective tool the Criminal Justice System does not use' (Restorative Justice Consortium, 2011).

The research literature provides a conflicting and ambivalent picture in relation to the successes and failures of conferencing. Therefore caution needs to be exercised at the micro level in acknowledging conferencing models and processes as an AOP in that the processes can equally empower and disempower participants and deny as well as create choices for individuals and families. This is also somewhat dependent on the YOT and the management philosophy of the department and the individual practitioner's view of conferencing. Previous research involving FGC in child protection cases highlighted that some social workers were resistant to making referrals and attending the intervention even though instructed to do so by organizational guidelines (Morris and Sheperd, 2000). This potentially is linked to feelings regarding the relinquishing of professional power and the capacity of families involved with social service departments (Morris and Sheperd, 2000; van Pagee, 2003).

At the macro level the context in which conference and the role of the facilitator operate may have a direct impact on how the intervention is implemented and therefore instrumental in transmitting power during the process while at the same time wider issues of structural power and oppression may go untouched (Beresford, 1988; Hugman, 1991; Ashley, 2008). The role of co-ordinator/facilitator is seen as vital and should be as independent as possible. However, in some local authorities these prerequisites could be undermined and exploited to achieve 'service' rather than 'needs' led outcomes (Essex County Council, 2004; Family Rights Group, 2007). In addition, the pressure to achieve government targets within ever-constricting financial budgets may compromise the integrity of the programme and therefore impact on the restorative outcomes of the process. Ultimately FGCs may not be financially viable resulting in the termination of the service. RJ is not welfare on the cheap; however, its legislative implementation in New Zealand coincided with the dual concerns of the overrepresentation of aboriginal youth in both the welfare and justice systems and also the costs of incarceration.

The failings of RJ have been written about extensively elsewhere and these are often associated with its unrealistic expectations as the panacea for all of society's ills (Fox, 2005, 2008). If funded and implemented correctly it is cost effective in the immediate and longer term with savings in relation to reduced social service and YJ involvement and where needed services are targeted and supportive rather than essentially mainstream (Shapland et al., 2011). It is culturally sensitive, empowering, resilient and strengths-based and provides a multidimensional intervention model that can transcend systemic resistance.

Conclusion

RJ interventions appear to have evolved to provide a useful alternative to the established practices of addressing criminal behaviour for adults and young people within the statutory justice system in the UK. Evidence that reinforces its effectiveness to satisfy the broad range of players in many criminal events, establish it as a viable alternative to the contemporary approaches in addressing offending behaviour.

However, one of many considerations and concerns relating to RJ is the inconsistency of practice implementation; this has rightly caused much debate among advocates and critics of RJ especially given its wholesale deployment with some of society's most vulnerable children, young people and their families. This concern is reflected in a sparse and ambivalent evidence base that presents contradictory messages in relation to a number of assumptions regarding the core processes and functions of restorative approaches.

The reflective practitioner will need to balance the many positive attributes of RJ with some of the less positive concerns. However, RJ, and specifically conferencing, remains a considerably progressive approach for workers who seek to engage service users with interventions and processes that are respectful, epitomize AOP and ADP and that seek to honour human rights and self-determination (Pitts, 1990; Payne, 2005).

EXERCISES

1   Using the case study on page x what alternative RJ outcomes could be identified for J as part of the Referral Order contract?

2   Do you think that there are certain crimes or particular offenders for whom RJ would not be suitable? If so, why?

Note

1   Shapland et al. (2011) give a comprehensive overview of the historical evolution of RJ practices in their book *Restorative Justice in Practice*.

10

High-risk offenders

LEARNING OUTCOMES

By the end of this chapter you should be able to:

* Understand the complex needs of high-risk offenders.

* Distinguish between different risks, characteristics and challenges posed in work and interventions with high-risk offenders.

* Reflect on the ethical dilemmas posed by work and interventions with high-risk offenders.

The conflicting values of the social work profession and those of the youth justice system (YJS) are no more apparent than in relation to high-risk offenders and the use of custody. Custody is in direct conflict with many aspects of the social work code of practice and code of ethics, but alternatives such as Intensive Supervision and Surveillance (ISS) (previously the Intensive Supervision and Surveillance Programme (ISSP) also provide ethical challenges for the practising social worker within the YJS. Additionally, at the structural and agency level in terms of YJS practice, the practitioner may often find sentencing options so prescribed that little is available as an alternative to custody. This in turn may impact on the social worker's personal and professional value base. This is especially relevant in relation to social justice and empowerment.

The complex needs of young people who commit serious offences or who are prolific offenders has been consistently highlighted by research (Arnull et al., 2005; Boswell, 1996). In response the YJB introduced the ISSP in 2001 to address serious offending in the community with the assistance of the latest technology, electronic tagging and intelligence-led policing. This was an acknowledgement that custody did not, and could not, meet the needs of high-risk young offenders. However, what all of the alternative programmes have in common is that they impose heavier penalties and stricter boundaries on the neediest and often most vulnerable young people. With the introduction of the Scaled Approach the programme became ISS and must now be considered for all young people at risk of custody; the court does not have to consult the Youth Offending Team (YOT) regarding suitability and can make a Youth Rehabilitation Order (YRO) with the ISS.

Intervening

This chapter should be read in conjunction with Chapter 6 (Intervention), as all that is said there relates also to this chapter. We consider some of the ways in which practitioners seek to engage and intervene with high-risk young people and think about the structures that are in place to support this; National Standards also guide the work with this group of young people. As mentioned in Chapter 4, some young people will be subject to the multidisciplinary surveillance of Multi-Agency Public Protection Arrangements (MAPPA), either because the nature of the offence they have committed is such as to mean that they must be referred (Categories 1 and 2) or because the practitioner's concerns about the risk they pose are such as to warrant referral (Category 3).

Other young people may also be said to pose a high level of risk but may not be subject to MAPPA or they may be subject to disposals but also under the surveillance of MAPPA. Such young people may have committed a violent or sexual offence that means they are automatically considered a high risk, or they may be prolific offenders committing multiple offences regularly.

Work being undertaken in the Youth Justice Board (YJB) at the moment is, as we discussed in Chapters 5 and 6, considering the possibility of moving away from the assessment tool (Asset) to a more flexible, practitioner-determined assessment, more akin to the diagnostic assessments undertaken on high-risk young people, which we now discuss.

Intensive Supervision and Surveillance (ISS)

The YJB says that ISS is designed to be 'a mixture of punishment and positive opportunities, available 365 days a year, providing the courts with a robust alternative to custody'. It can have reparative elements, seek to address criminogenic factors and work with the young person to put structures in place to encourage desistance. Like MAPPA, ISS seeks to '... manage the risks posed by the young person to the community' and to reintegrate the young person into their community through their engagement in activities that will continue post-supervision.

ISS can be used pre-sentencing/conviction and post-conviction; it can form a condition of bail where the young person might be remanded into custody; it can be attached to a YRO, or form a condition of a Notice of Supervision on release from custody. There are three bands of ISS: band 1 high intensity; band 2 medium intensity; and band 3 extended ISS. All have different levels of contact and the latter has different electronic monitoring arrangements; because of their complexity you should consult National Standards.

ISS is designed to have core elements composed of offending behaviour and restorative justice work, education, training and employment (ETE), interpersonal skills work and family support elements. As with other sentences in the YJS it addresses a number of elements in a young person's life. Therefore while the very nature of ISS appears to be derived from a justice model, its incorporation of work to address social and family needs and structural deficits suggests that it also draws on welfare models, and adds to this complexity by also including restorative approaches.

ISS interventions are intense with high levels of supervision; for example, in the 6-month programme a young person will have 25 hours contact per week in the first 3 months and then 5 hours per week for a further 3 months. A 12-month programme follows a similar trajectory but with 25 hours contact lasting for 4 months and with total contact hours within the year totalling 2,601.

Persistent, prolific or frequent – young offenders

ISS was developed to target young people who were appearing in court and who had been charged, warned or convicted of offences on four or more separate dates within a period of 12 months and who had previously received a custodial or community sentence, or where an offence was likely to lead to a sentence of imprisonment, which for an adult could lead to 14 years or more. High risk is therefore taken to imply seriousness and/or frequency. Terminology in the Youth Justice (YJ) sector fluctuates and is subject to 'fashion', thus around frequency of offending it has varied over the years and has been termed 'persistent' and 'prolific'; this is true in other areas too, with 'vulnerable' now referred to as 'the young person's safety'. What has remained common and constant have been the concerns about young people who commit a high frequency of offences, but as for other high-risk groups they are uncommon and therefore there has been a sustained attempt to better understand and respond to this population. As a way of doing this, in 2005 the YJB commissioned one of the authors of this book (Arnull et al., 2005) to look retrospectively at 'persistent' young offenders (PYO) in order to help draw a picture of what they 'looked like' and what events had happened to them in their lives prior to their persistent offending. The research involved talking to young people and YOT practitioners, but also gave access to social services records and thus a detailed retrospective picture could be built. The findings were that this population were distinct from the general YOT population and that:

- a history of family disruption was more pronounced than for the general YOT population with higher levels of bereavement, abuse and violence within a family setting. For example, almost half of the sample had some form of recorded abuse;
- much higher levels of being 'looked after' – 38 per cent of the sample compared with 0.5 per cent of the general population;
- high levels of offending with family and friends – 45 per cent of the sample;
- low educational attainment and engagement – 45 per cent of the sample were regular truants;
- higher levels of mental ill health and drug and alcohol use, although the latter was rarely related to offending and appeared for some at least to have been self-medication.

In terms of offending, the young people committed a high volume of offences, many of which were not serious, but some of which were – including robbery and violence.

Breach rates were also high suggesting the young people were hard to engage, and when interviewed they said the key element in their positive engagement was the relationship they formed with the supervising adult. The caution to custody window was short and the age at first caution was a year and a half earlier than in a study by Baker et al. (2003) of the general YOT population. Although the relationship was not established it is probable that the frequency of offending and poor engagement were contributory factors. As a retrospective study it is limited by being only able to describe those already in the YJS, and thus it is not possible to know how many similar young people managed to forge successful, non-offending lives. However, the high frequency of those from at risk populations suggests there is a link with difficult and structurally impoverished lives that makes it harder for young people to achieve this. Furthermore, the PYO' study does give an accurate picture of the factors that have affected high-frequency young offenders and is consistent with other research in this area; the messages from it therefore are ones that are important for practitioners.

The authors found little evidence that practitioners integrated or had knowledge of past interventions, recording was patchy, and there was limited inter-agency work. The authors discussed how they would have expected to see a history of targeted, intensive interventions aimed at the range of needs, vulnerabilities and offending of this group of young people but what they found was that 'no evidence of a planned intervention for a clearly identified need, with anticipated outcomes and where those outcomes had been recorded' (Arnull et al., 2005: 7). We noted that this was in keeping with other studies and this has remained a consistent and hard to shift feature within YOTs with the Inspection Report (IYO/CJJI, 2011) showing the same pattern and lack of clarity.

The evaluation of the pilots of the ISSP found that the 12-month programme largely targeted young people who had committed a serious offence (50 per cent), rather than those with high levels of need or who were frequent offenders (20 per cent) and sentencers suggested they used offence seriousness as a key indicator. This profile was different from the six-month programme that had mainly targeted frequent offenders (i.e. more similar to the PYO study); although in both samples 25 per cent were both frequent and serious offenders. The levels of underlying need in the six-month ISSP sample are very similar to the profile of persistent offenders shown above, but those of the serious offenders in the 12-month sample showed less serious levels of underlying need (see also Arnull and Eagle, 2009). It was posited that the lower levels of underlying need in the serious but not frequent offenders made it much harder for the ISSP as there were fewer issues for practitioners to intervene with and breach occurred in the latter stages of the orders as a result. The results suggest therefore a difference in the characteristics of serious offenders and frequent offenders, although both pose a risk due to the nature of their offending. The findings suggest therefore that different sorts of responses are required for each group.

ISSP was found to be a direct alternative to custody with 91 per cent of those for whom it was recommended and who did not receive it going into custody. The 12-month programme was found to be highly intrusive, however, with high levels of surveillance and monitoring; the evaluators described it as 'the most intensive and intrusive community programme ever made available for young offenders in England and Wales' (2007b: 14).

The authors of the evaluation concluded that the programme was not effective with serious offenders as currently designed and should only be used with those whose offending was serious and frequent.

Intensive Fostering Programme

Another programme aimed at diverting children and young people who are assessed as posing a high risk and therefore likely to be sentenced to custody is the Intensive Fostering Programme (IFP) which was based on a cognitive behavioural therapy (CBT) model developed in the USA in the 1980s. The YJB (2010a: 84) says that is aimed at '. . . children and young people whose home life is felt to have contributed significantly to their offending behaviour' and it therefore seeks to remove them from that environment but enables them to remain in the community while addressing their offending behaviour and improving their social skills. The schemes became available in the Criminal Justice and Immigration Act (2008) as an alternative to custody and form part of a YRO. A young person can remain in the IFP for up to 12 months and at the same time a programme of support can be offered to their family, including family therapy, counselling and parenting skills. While the young person is in the IFP the foster carer will be in daily contact with the young person's YOT practitioner to discuss behaviour patterns and to seek to identify and address any issues before they become critical.

While the scheme is based on CBT and involves points and levels to reward desired behaviour, it also seeks to engage with wider social and structural deficits in order to support the young person and encourage their desistance from offending.

Dangerousness and serious specified offences

Young offenders can no longer simply be sentenced to an indeterminate sentence as had been the case in the past by a judge on the basis of the seriousness of their offence. The Criminal Justice Act 2003 and its subsequent amendments in the Criminal Justice and Immigration Act 2008 provide the legal framework for Assessments of Dangerousness by courts who consider a young person of such high risk that a life or indeterminate sentence should be made; these assessments are then undertaken by the YOT.

The practitioner undertakes the assessment and can draw on information held by a range of agencies, and may also include allegations of harm or dangerousness held by the police for example, but which may not have formed a conviction. They can build up a pattern or a suggestion of a pattern of behaviour, based on convictions and allegations of criminal or risky behaviour, along with other information and knowledge about the young person, but clearly the ethical implications and challenges need to be fully thought through. In so doing the practitioner needs to utilize all of their social work skills, reflection and ethics to ensure that the judgements they form are Anti-Oppressive (AO) and Anti-Discriminatory (AD) and take a rounded and holistic view of all the information available and the young person subject to the assessment.

The practitioner then considers the risk posed by the young person and forms a judgement and the report is submitted, but only the court can determine whether or not a young person is held to be 'dangerous' and if they are whether a Detention for Life, Detention for Public Protection (DPP), or Extended Sentence, or any other available sentence can be passed. A young person or adult offender can only be considered dangerous if 'the court is of the opinion that there is a significant risk to members of the public of serious harm occasioned by the commission by him of further specified offences' (CJA 2003).

Since 2008 a conviction for a specified offence, which might make you the subject of MAPPA, does not in itself lead to a presumption of dangerousness, but where the criteria are met or the young person is found guilty of the specified offence by a youth court they must then be committed to the Crown Court for sentence; at the Crown Court an assessment of dangerousness will be undertaken. Additionally, if the offence does not merit a custodial period of at least two years, even if there are convictions for Schedule 15A offences, the young offender may not be sentenced, if found to be dangerous, to either an indeterminate sentence or an extended sentence. The legislation around this area is detailed and complex, however, and because most practitioners will deal with assessments of dangerousness intermittently, expert advice and guidance from the court and the legal representatives should always be sought.

Once the assessment is completed if the court does consider the young person dangerous and they are able to make a DPP and do so, they must state the minimum term that can be served before a parole board gives consideration as to whether or not the young person can safely be released from custody; once released they will be subject to an Indefinite Licence that is subject to review after 10 years.

Summary

The key issues with which you need to get to grips are the different conceptions around high risk. Those focus in particular on frequency and dangerousness/seriousness and the two cohorts of young offenders are in general distinct, presenting with different issues and needs. Young people who are high-frequency offenders display a high level of needs, some of which are criminogenic and some not. Serious offenders, or those termed 'dangerous', may not present with the same level of general needs and will not require the same level of intervention, although they may require containment or surveillance. The ISS programme was designed to address the needs of high-frequency offenders; the evaluation suggests its design of multi-faceted programmes with high levels of contact did meet the needs of this group. However, they found that as currently designed it does not meet the needs of those who are infrequent but serious offenders.

EXERCISES

1   How does the notion of indeterminate sentencing for children and young people sit with the British Association of Social Work (BASW) code of ethics and the HCPC code of conduct in relation to engaging service users?

2   What interventions would you employ to engage non-compliant and uncooperative young people? You might want to draw on ideas from Chapters 9 and 11.

11

Alternative interventions

Contributing author: Megan Bunting, Arts Practitioner

LEARNING OBJECTIVES

By the end of this chapter you should be able to:

*   Understand the types of alternative interventions that can be offered to young offenders.

*   Reflect upon the importance of 'soft skills' development and how it can aid re-habilitation.

*   Comprehend the challenges and advantages posed by undertaking small-scale research on YJ practice.

This chapter examines alternative interventions, with a particular focus on creative methods for working with young offenders or those at risk of offending in a Youth Offending Team (YOT) setting. The author as both a drama practitioner and researcher has worked on various arts programmes with YOTs, and uses her own experience and research as the foundation for this chapter. The chapter is laid out in three parts: the first part introduces alternative artistic approaches, and the background for their use in the YJS; the second part focuses on research undertaken by the author as part of a Master in Community Sectoral Arts programme and an additional project that developed from that piece of academic research; and the third part there are exercises offered and additional reference websites identified that can be used to assist in developing arts programmes within a YOT setting.

Introduction

Many artists and arts organizations have experience of working in the youth criminal justice system (CJS) in the UK but for the purposes of this chapter, only the two that were mentioned by the YOT employees surveyed as part of the research project are highlighted.

Two companies that have influenced drama work with young offenders in England and Wales are Theatre in Prison and Probation (TiPP) and Geese Theatre Company UK. What is unique about these companies is not only do they create their own arts-based work specifically for the criminal justice system but they train employees within the criminal justice system (i.e. probation officers, YOT practitioners, prison officers) to help them deliver work in their own settings.

TiPP is now a registered charity but was previously based within the University of Manchester's Drama Department. Their belief is that 'theatre and related arts have the power to transform lives' (TiPP, 2012). Their first major project was an offending-based drama workshop called *Blagg*! Based on the fictional character, Jo Blagg, the group uses drama exercises and role-play scenarios to create Jo Blagg's history, criminal offence(s) and future as a result. Time is taken to examine the point of view of the victim and what changes could be made to prevent offending. The first *Blagg*! programmes delivered in partnership with two YOTs in the north west of England were evaluated extensively in *Blagg*! Evaluation Report by the Centre of Applied Theatre Research (2003). The report is a good example of working in partnership, using thorough evaluation procedures and adapting arts work to reflect the issues raised from the evaluation. TiPP continues to run training workshops to enable those who work with challenging young people to deliver the *Blagg*! programme themselves.

The Geese Theatre Company UK was formed in 1987 as a sister organization to the Geese Theatre USA (Baim et al., 2002). Their approach as described on their website is: 'The company believes that drama is a powerful and effective vehicle for inviting individuals to examine their own behaviour and as a catalyst for promoting personal development and change' (Geese Theatre UK, 2012).

The Geese Theatre Company has a specialized style of working, usually with the medium of masks, which is underpinned by drama therapy methods. However, they offer training for employees working in the CJS in groupwork using drama skills. The Geese Theatre Company has also produced a handbook of exercises and groupwork ideas based on their methods for practitioners working in the CJS, in conflict settings or theatre environments.

Background information

Within the UK there has been a growing acceptance of utilizing the arts as a means of engaging challenging young people and since 2002 the Arts Council of England (ACE) and the Youth Justice Board (YJB) have recognized this and have worked together to provide effective arts projects within the sector. Momentum for arts interventions increased in 2005 when the Arts Council outlined its national strategy 'Arts and Young People at Risk of Offending' (Arts Council England, 2005). The strategy aimed to help young people at risk of offending to:

- develop their interest and skills in the arts;
- challenge their views of themselves and raise their aspirations;
- engage with learning;

- connect with new education, training and employment opportunities; and
- make a positive contribution to society.

In 2006, the ACE and the YJB formed a strategic partnership and as a result many creative approaches were used to address offending behaviour. One result was the development of Summer Arts Colleges that built on the Summer Splash scheme. This in time evolved into Splash Extra and then into Positive Activities for Young People (PAYP) (CRG Research Ltd, 2007: 2). PAYP continues to grow and is now managed by the Department of Culture, Media and Sport (DCMS, 2012) with a focus on streamlining funding in order to improve access to the programmes for young people. The Summer Arts Colleges aim to provide education and training activities using the arts as a delivery method during the school summer holidays. They are co-funded by the ACE, the YJB (and since 2011 Youth Music), and are run by YOTs with support from the charity Unitas (YJB, 2010c) which quality assures the schemes. The Summer Arts Colleges work with those young people either on Detention Training Orders (DTOs) or on the Intensive Supervision and Surveillance (ISS) and offer a nationally recognized Arts Award qualification at bronze or silver level upon completion.

Research

Rationale

Prior to the implementation of the Summer Arts Colleges, YOTs were already using arts as an alternative method of engaging with young people. I was interested in ascertaining to what degree these approaches were being utilized and therefore in 2006, as part of an MA in Community Sectoral Arts programme, I undertook a qualitative dissertation study examining how and why these arts programmes were being used.

Findings

Each individual arts programme was unique to the YOT that delivered it and the research uncovered no overlap between teams. Some factors that contributed to how the YOT delivered the project were: location (rural or urban), national, regional and local initiatives, budget, access to funding, access to partners, client need, motivation and talent within the team (Bunting, 2006). These factors influenced whether programmes were delivered frequently or infrequently, on a one-to-one basis or in a group, if the group was mixed gender or not, size of the group, level of risk, the art form used and who delivered it. A common theme was that although there was not one way to incorporate or deliver arts programmes with young offenders, there was a right way suitable to each YOT.

Here are some examples of art forms used to work with young people drawn from interviews with YOT workers:

- The arts project had originally been piloted using drama and was not 100 per cent successful as a result. This was because this medium is difficult to use on a one-to-one basis and therefore it was opened up to various other media as a form of engagement.

- I think drama has a great way of engaging people who have been excluded, who may have difficulty expressing themselves and who may not often have the opportunity to participate.

- Literature/poetry/rap – language examination from the East End, Cockney rhyming slang. Examining how sometimes what we say sometimes doesn't make sense!

- [The aims of the project were] addressed using drama at first, writing pieces with the young people and then we looked at other art forms – the work was young person led.

- The kids created posters with a restorative justice theme called 'Victims Count'.

The Crime and Disorder Act 1998, s. 37, states 'it shall be the principal aim of the youth justice system to prevent offending by children and young persons' and this was the main reason cited for using arts activities with young people (Bunting, 2006). A secondary reason was the benefits that young people receive from the programmes; for example, building self-esteem, discovering hidden talent, accessing learning skills, sense of achievement, developing social skills and confidence-building. These 'soft skills' are sometimes harder to evaluate but are clearly observed by those who work with young offenders on arts activities. Interestingly, the Unitas evaluation reports for the Summer Arts Colleges do not look at 'soft skill' development, but focus on attendance and participation, offending rates, literacy and numeracy skill development and whether an arts award had been achieved. It would be interesting to evaluate the 'soft skills' as they can be just as important in assisting with reducing offending and training and education pursuits (Blades et al., 2012; House of Commons Education and Skills Committee, 2005).

Hughes (2005) reviewed the literature and practices in arts work with offenders in the report *Doing the Arts Justice*, and found a broad range of challenging and relevant arts-based practices within the CJS and the youth CJS that met educational, artistic, therapeutic and artistic aims. The main weakness highlighted was the lack of sufficient evidence about these criminal justice arts practices specifically when examining participation in the arts making a difference to the participant. The final emergent theme from the dissertation research identified the lack of evaluation in relation to programmes used by YOTs. This has been somewhat addressed by Unitas which in its appraisal of projects now considers reduction of offending, although unfortunately does not extend this to how the arts programmes impact on the participants personally (Adams, 2012; Tarling and Adams, 2012).

A summary of the research outcomes were that the arts programmes were varied and needed to be suitable to each individual YOT. The reasons for incorporating arts projects into the service were to prevent further offending and to provide 'soft skill' benefits to the participants. Finally, there were insufficient evaluations being conducted to examine the impact of using the arts with young offenders. These outcomes influenced the development of an arts project 'in-fusion' that utilized both research findings and artistic skills in a practical application within a YOT setting.

An example of an arts project: in-fusion

To explain how an arts project may work in a YOT, personal experience of working on a three-year arts project that was delivered in partnership with two YOTs and its progession from an academic MA dissertation project into a funded research project will be shared. For the purposes of confidentiality aspects of the project have been anonymized.

The history

Initially, the arts programme 'in-fusion' was developed and delivered as a pilot project in December 2005 with a London Youth Offending Service (YOS). As a result of the Every Child Matter's (ECM) Green Paper (2004), which outlined five core aims for young people receiving government services: '(1) Be Healthy; (2) Stay Safe; (3) Enjoy and Achieve; (4) Make a Positive Contribution; and (5) Achieve Economic Well-being', some members of the YOT had undertaken training from the National Children's Bureau regarding the 'make a positive contribution' aim of ECM. More specifically, how to encourage young people who receive government services to feed back and improve those services (Ministry of Justice, 2008: 59). The aim proved challenging for the YOT members as they struggled to establish a method to glean this information from young people who were obliged to receive their service. At the same time, I was undertaking my MA and needed an opportunity to practise what I was learning. I had a contact working within this YOT who mentioned this conundrum and offered the use of my drama skills as a possible solution.

The YOT chose certain young offenders (selected from a spectrum of court orders, which encompassed various ethnic backgrounds and both genders) in a one-off workshop using theatre-based skills to see if they could come together as a group. If the original workshop was successful, further sessions would be planned. In acknowledgement of their participation the young offenders exchanged two hours attendance, and received four hours counted as reparation served. The result was a successful creation of a team of young offenders and YOT officers, who thoughtfully contributed to the improvement of the service.

I completed my academic studies which incorporated the outcomes of the pilot project. I arranged to meet with the Head of Prevention at the YJB to discuss the findings and to explore the idea of developing the project to engage with a greater number of YOTs and consequently more young people. While he was supportive of the work, the importance of evidencing the results in a more systematic manner was stressed. I therefore undertook fund-raising opportunities that were successful and allowed for an external evaluator to be hired from a local university to accompany the arts programme into its augmented next phase. To extend the reach of this project it was named 'in-fusion' and a London-based arts in criminal justice charity was engaged to assist with the project management and promotion of this venture.

The aim

The aim of this programme was to work with the YOTs in providing a drama-based programme that engaged young offenders to participate in contributing to the YOS.

The programme met the aim by utilizing drama games, role-play exercises and participatory techniques to achieve the following objectives:

- To receive objective feedback from the young offenders about the service provided by the YOT.
- To empower young people by encouraging their positive contributions and including them to make a difference.
- To strengthen the relationships between the YOT officers and the young offenders.
- To disseminate the suggestions/feedback made by the group.
- To provide access to drama skills.
- To develop social skills for young people.
- To meet the positive contribution aim of the ECM agenda.

Who was the arts programme for?

The programme was aimed at young offenders and young ex-offenders (14–18) and YOT officers. It was designed for those interested in sharing their views and participating in improving the services of their local YOT. Seventy-five per cent of the participants were young offenders while 25 per cent were staff. The YOT worked closely with the project team to identify the most suitable participants and help to ensure the success of the delivery.

The content

Drama was the core of the programme delivery with the use of video to record the outcomes. Permission slips were issued for participants to agree to being recorded. Groupwork methods were dynamic to encourage direct participation from the participants through practical drama exercises. The programme was delivered in four sessions each lasting two hours, with a follow-up fifth session three months later. Part of the programme was determined by the participants depending on what medium they chose to reflect their feedback of the YOS (see Table 11.1).

Evaluation

An external evaluator focused on two areas of analysis: the programme process and the programme as intervention. The study sought data from staff and from the participating young people and used a qualitative and quantitative mixed-method approach.

Outcomes

Several YOTs were approached and one in the eastern region agreed to participate with the project, specifying that they wanted to focus on the rural part of their county as this was often overlooked when interesting opportunities occurred. Further funding

Table 11.1 Drama session and activity programme example

Session	Activities
1	Create a solid team and build trust through the use of quick drama games and exercises
2	Role-play scenarios • Young offenders to play magistrates in court while the YOT officers to play young offenders • *What happens when you visit the YOT* – young offenders to play officers and YOT officers to play young offenders Group discussions as a result leading to feedback about the YOT service
3	Group decision as to how the participants want to project their feedback to the YOT; options include: • Drama performance, video diary, letter to the manager, any other suggestions from the participants Begin work on the presentation of the feedback
4	Finalize work on the feedback presentation The final work to be video-recorded as part of the evaluation
5	Follow-up session three months later: • Viewing of the recorded work • Group discussions: has anything changed? Feedback about the programme

became available and additional partnerships with an urban YOT in London were developed as well. This allowed work with the rural YOT twice and the urban YOT once; on each occasion this enabled improvements to be made to the delivery and further data for the final evaluation to be gained. The evaluation reports came in three phases: a thorough examination of each programme delivered for each YOT and then a comparison report identifying what worked and what needed improvement.

The evaluation revealed the process was largely successful. The relationship between the young people and the YOT officers improved as a result of the team-building and problem-solving exercises and food during breaks allowed informal relationship development. All of the young people enjoyed the drama activities and some recognized the transferability of the skills and increased their confidence.

Critique

Although this was a small-scale research project whose inception was inspired by an MA dissertation, the resounding message from the findings was that improvement was required in disseminating the feedback the young people provided, back to the YOT. One of the programmes only had one YOT officer for the final feedback session and that officer was a sessional employee. Interestingly, Unitas implemented an online survey system for the Summer Arts Colleges in 2011, to seek feedback from the young people participating (Unitas, 2012). What happens to that feedback or how it will be used to influence programme development is unclear.

For both the urban and rural programmes, when we met again three months later to examine whether anything had changed, the answer was consistently 'no', nothing had changed. This could be seen as a tokenistic gesture by the YOT to participate in the arts project, if no suggestions were incorporated into the service. This in turn raised a number of questions:

1   Was this aspect of the programme too aspirational?
2   Were YOT staff too overstretched to even think about incorporating change?
3   Was there further support we could have provided the YOT to ensure that the changes were seen through?

There was a lot of time spent together to form solid groups who felt comfortable and equal in their discussions and at the end of the project the message back to the young people was that their voices did not matter. This theme appeared structurally symptomatic of the YJB as no response was received from the Head of Prevention at the YJB after the evaluation reports had been sent to him. This is interesting given the route that the YJB has now taken in terms of its arts programming and the use of Unitas.

Although quite a disappointing ending to a very rewarding arts project, it still provided options of how to improve arts programming with young offenders. It also reinforced the earlier dissertation research findings that not all arts projects worked in all YOTs; they often are site and/or person/worker-specific (see gender-based work in Arnull and Eagle, 2009). More importantly, it highlighted that both management support and that of practitioners engaged in one-on-one work was crucial. Artists can provide the means to assist in developing skills for young people in the youth CJS, but there needs to be opportunities for young people to practise these skills.

Conclusion

Arts work has a place in the youth criminal justice setting and has proven to be a successful method of engagement. Throughout this chapter research has been used to highlight that arts projects are mainly used for reduction of offending purposes and for 'soft skill' development. Current practices have been compared by focusing on Unitas and the Summer Arts Colleges where reducing offending, training and education seem to be the focus but the personal impact on the participant is not being evaluated. Personal experiences of one particular YOT arts project have been imparted where the evaluation was considered the most important aspect but unfortunately was not utilized to improve services once the findings had been disseminated.

Participating in an arts programme can be highly rewarding for both participants and practitioners. As a practitioner, if you are interested in using creative interventions, it is recommended that you attempt them. If creative approaches are not a personal strength, then consider working alongside arts companies and practitioners that can either train you or deliver an arts project for you. As the above research and practice has shown, keeping the arts project YOT- and staff-specific will help ensure success alongside an evaluation process that is used as the foundation to improve future work.

EXERCISE

Create an arts project for your team. Decide whether the project is for one-to-one work or for a group setting. What considerations need to be addressed in order to ensure success?

Useful websites

1   The Arts Alliance: www.artsalliance.ning.com
2   Geese Theatre Company: www.geese.co.uk
3   Theatre in Prison and Probation (TiPP): www.tipp.org.uk
4   Rideout: www.rideout.org.uk
5   Dance United: www.dance-united.com
6   Clean Break: www.cleanbreak.org.uk
7   Unitas: www.unitas.uk.net
8   Escape Artists: www.escapeartists.co.uk

Bibliography

Adams, M. (2012) *Summer Arts Colleges Outcomes Report 2011*. Available online at www.unitas. uk.net/Assets/305224/Document.pdf?1339763848

Ammar, N.H. (2001) Restorative justice in Islam: theory and practice, in Michael L. Hadley (ed.) *The Spiritual Roots of Restorative Justice* (pp. 161–81). New York: State University of New York.

Anderson, B., Beinart, S., Farrington, D., Langman, J., Sturgis, P. and Utting, D. (2005) *Risk and Protective Factors*. London. Youth Justice Board for England and Wales.

Andrews, D.A. and Dowden, C. (2006) Risk principle of case classification in correctional treatment: a meta-analytic investigation, *International Journal of Offender Therapy and Comparative Criminology*, 50: 88–100.

Andrews, D.A., Bonta, J. and Wormith, S.J. (2006) The recent past and near future of risk and/ or need assessment, *Crime and Delinquency*, 52: 7–27.

Arnull, E. (1998) Crime, drugs and young people, *Criminal Justice Matters*, 31 (2): 21–23.

Arnull, E. (2007) *The development and implementation of drug policy in England 1994–2004*, published thesis, Middlesex University.

Arnull, E. (2008) The performance management of drug policy, *Journal of Drugs, Education, Prevention and Policy*, Autumn.

Arnull, E. (2012a) That is not it at all: unintended effects and policy outcomes. Unpublished manuscript, London Metropolitan University.

Arnull, E. (2012b) Social work and the youth justice system: ensuring social work values. Paper presented at the International Association of Schools of Social Work, Stockholm, Sweden.

Arnull, E. and Eagle, S. (2009) *Girls and Offending – Patterns, Perceptions and Interventions*. London: Youth Justice Board for England and Wales.

Arnull, E., Eagle, S., Gammampila, A., Miller, K. and Archer, D. (2005) *A Retrospective Study of Persistent Young Offenders*. Final Report to Youth Justice Board. London: Youth Justice Board for England and Wales.

Arnull, E., Eagle, S., Gammampila, A., Patel, S.L. and Sadler, J. (2007) *The Accommodation Needs and Experiences of Young Offenders*. London: Youth Justice Board for England and Wales.

Arts Council England (2005) The Arts and Young People at Risk of Offending. Available online at www.artscouncil.org.uk/media/uploads/documents/publications/youngpeopleatriskpdf_ phpaQu2aP.pdf

Arts Council England (2012) *Publications Section*. Available online at www.artscouncil.org.uk/ publication_archive/doing-the-arts-justice-a-review-of-research-literature-practice-and-theory/

Ashley, C. (2008) Lost in the short cuts, *Community Care*, 2008:8.

Audit Commission (1996) *Misspent Youth: Young People and Crime*. London: Audit Commission.

Baim, C., Brookes, S. and Mountford, A. (eds) (2002) *The Geese Theatre Handbook*. Winchester: Waterside Press.

Baker, K. (2005) Assessment in youth justice: professional discretion and the use of Asset, *Youth Justice*, 5(2): 106–12.

Baker, K. (2007) Risk, uncertainty and public protection: assessment of young people who offend, *British Journal of Social Work Online*, 31 July.

Baker, K., Jones, S., Roberts, C. and Merrington, S. (2003) Further development of Asset: interim report. Unpublished manuscript.

Ballucci, D. (2008) Risk in action: the practical effect of youth management assessment, *Social & Legal Studies*, 17(2): 175–97.

Barnard, A. (ed.) (2011) *Key Themes in Health and Social Care: A Companion to Learning*. Abingdon: Routledge.

Barnes, V. (2011) Social work and advocacy with young people: rights and care in practice, *British Journal of Social Work*. Published online 5 October.

Bazemore, G. (1999) After shaming, whither reintegration: restorative justice and relational rehabilitation, in G. Bazemore and L. Walgrave (eds) *Restorative Juvenile Justice: Repairing the Harm of Youth Crime*. Monsey, NY: Criminal Justice Press.

BBC (1999) Child prostitute 'failed' by social workers, Monday, 4 October. Published at 15:17 GMT 16:17 UK at www.news.bbc.co.uk/1/hi/uk/464224.stm (accessed 8 October 2012).

BBC News (2009) *UK Society 'Condemning' Children*. Available online at www.news.bbc.co.uk/1/hi/7732290.stm (accessed 1 October 2009).

Beart, K., Whitehead, G. and Barnard, A. (2011) Working with people, in A. Barnard (ed.) *Key Themes in Health and Social Care: A Companion to Learning*. London: Routledge.

Beck, J.S. with Beck, A. (2011) *Cognitive Behavior Therapy: Basics and Beyond* (2nd edn). New York: Guilford Press.

Becker, H.S. (1963) *Outsiders: Studies in the Sociology of Deviance*. London: Macmillan.

Beresford, P. (1988) Consumer views: data collection or democracy?, in I. Allen (ed) *Hearing the Voice of the Consumer*. London: Policy Studies Institute.

Beresford, P. (2010) Service users and social policy: developing different discussions, challenging dominant discourses, *Social Policy Review*, 22: 227–52.

Berg, I. and Steiner, T. (2003) *Children's Solution Work*. New York: W.W. Norton.

Berzin, S.C., Cohen, E., Thomas, K. and Dawson, W.C. (2008) Does family group decision making affect child welfare outcomes? Findings from a randomized control study, *Child Welfare*, 87(4): 35–54.

Best, S. (2005) *Understanding Social Divisions*. London: Sage Publications.

Blades, R., Fauth, B. and Gibb, J. (2012) *Measuring Employability Skills: A Rapid Review to inform development of tools for project evaluation*, National Children's Bureau. Available online at www.ncb.org.uk/media/579980/measuring_employability_skills_final_report_march2012.pdf

Blagg, H. (2001) Aboriginal youth and restorative justice: critical notes from the Australian frontier, in A. Morris and G. Maxwell (eds) *Restoring Justice for Juveniles: Conferences, Mediation and Circles*. Oxford. Hart Publishing.

Blyth, M. and Solomon, E. (2009) *Prevention and Youth Crime: Is Early Intervention Working?* Bristol: Policy Press.

Boswell, G. (1996) *Young and Dangerous: The Backgrounds and Careers of Section 53 Offenders* Brookfield, VT: Avebury Publishing Co.

Braithwaite, J. (1998) Restorative justice, in M. Tonry (ed.) *The Handbook of Crime and Punishment* (pp. 323–44). New York: Oxford University Press.

Brayne, H. and Carr, H. (2008) *Law for Social Workers* (9th edn). Oxford: Oxford University Press.

British Association of Social Workers (BASW) (2012) *A Code of Ethics for Social Work*. Available online at www.basw.co.uk/about/code-of-ethics/ (accessed 22 August 2011).

Brofenbrenner, U. (1979) *The Ecology of Human Development: Experiments by Nature and Design*. Cambridge, MA: Harvard University Press.

Brown, A. (1997) Groupwork, in M. Davis (ed.) *The Blackwell Companion to Social Work* (pp. 223–30). Oxford: Blackwell Publishers.

Bryan, K., Freer, J. and Furlong, C. (2007) Language and communication difficulties in juvenile offenders, *International Journal of Language and Communication Disorders*, 42: 505–20.

Bunting, M. (2006) How is it working? An examination of arts programme delivery in youth offending services across England and Wales. Unpublished MA dissertation.

Burke, B. and Harrison, P. (2002) Anti-oppressive practice, in R. Adams, L. Dominelli and M. Payne (eds) *Social Work* (pp. 227–36). Basingstoke: Palgrave Macmillan.

Burnett, R. and Appleton, C. (2004) Joined-up services to tackle youth crime: a case study in England, *British Journal of Criminology*, 44: 34–54.

Burney, E. (2006) 'No Spitting': regulation of offensive behaviour in England and Wales in A. Von Hirsch and A.P. Simester (eds). *Incivilities: Regulating Offensive Behaviour* (pp. 195–219). Oxford: Hart Publishing.

Butler, I. (2002) A code of ethics for social work and social care research, *British Journal of Social Work*, 32: 239–48.

Carlin, E. (undated) *Feeling Good: Supporting Resilience in Young People in Foyers in England*. London: Foyer Federation.

Cavadino, M. and Dignan, J. (2005) *The Penal System: An Introduction*. London: Sage Publications.

Centre for Applied Theatre Research (2003) *The Impact of Blagg on Challenging and Reducing Offending by Young People: An Evaluation of a Drama Based Offending Behaviour Workshop*. Available online at www.tipp.org.uk/tipp/index.php?page=research

Children and Young People Now (2011) *Deadline Missed on Young Offender Education*. Available online at www.cypnow.co.uk/Education/article/1074688/deadline-missed-young-offender-education/ (accessed 14 July 2011).

Clifford, D. and Burke, B. (2004) Moral and professional dilemmas in long-term assessment of children and families, *Journal of Social Work*, 4(3): 305–21. London: Sage Publications.

Community Justice Forum (1998) *Canadian Resource Guide: Royal Canadian Mounted Police*. Canada: Minster Public Works and Government Services.

Cook, D. and Hudson, B. (1993) *Racism and Criminology*. Thousand Oaks, CA: Sage Publications.

Cormack, E. (1996) *Women in Trouble*. Halifax: Fernwood.

Coulshed, V. (1991) Social Work Practice: *An Introduction*. Basingstoke: Macmillan/BASW.

Coussee, F., Roets, G. and De Bie, M. (2009) Empowering the powerful: challenging hidden processes of marginalisation in youth work policy and practice in Belgium, *Critical Social Policy*, 29(3): 421–42.

Crawford, A. and Newburn, T. (2002) Recent developments in restorative justice for young people in England and Wales: community participation and representation, *British Journal of Criminology*, 42: 476–95.

Crawford, A. and Newburn, T. (2003) *Youth Offending and Restorative Justice: Implementing Reform in Youth Justice*. Devon: Willan Publishing.

Cree, V. (2010) *Sociology for Social Workers and Probation Officers* (2nd edn). London: Routledge.

CRG Research Ltd (2007) *Positive Activities for Young People: A National Evaluation*. Available online at www.education.gov.uk/publications/eOrderingDownload/CRG-01998–2006.pdf

Cullen, F.T., Maakestad, W.J. and Cavender, G. (1987) *Corporate Crime Under Attack: The Ford Pinto Case and Beyond*. Cincinnati, OH: Anderson.

Cunningham. J. and Cunningham. S. (2008) *Sociology and Social Work*. Exeter: Learning Matters.

Dallos, R. and Draper, R. (2000) *An Introduction to Family Therapy*. Maideahead: Open University Press.

Daly, K. (2001) Conferencing in Australia and New Zealand: variations, research findings and prospects, in A. Morris and G. Maxwell (eds) *Restoring Justice for Juveniles: Conferences, Mediation and Circles*. Oxford: Hart Publishing.

Daly, K. and Immarigeon, R. (1998) The past, present, and future of restorative justice: some critical reflections, *Contemporary Justice Review*, 1(1): 21–45.

Davies, J.S. (2002) Regeneration partnerships under New Labour: a case of creeping centralisation, in C. Glendinning, M. Powell and K. Rummery (eds) *Partnerships, New Labour and the Governance of Welfare*. Bristol: Policy Press.

Delgrado, R. (2000) Prosecuting violence: a colloquy on race, community and justice, goodbye to Hammuarabi: analysing the atavistic appeal of restorative justice, *Stanford Law Review*, 52: 751–75.

Department of Culture, Media and Sport (2012) *PAYP FAQs*. Available online at www.culture. gov.uk/what_we_do/education_and_social_policy/4108.aspx

Department of Education (2011) *Positive for Youth: A New Approach to Cross-Government Policy for Young People Aged 13 to 19*. London: HMSO.

De Shazer, S. (2003). *'Don't Think, But Observe': What is the Importance of the Work of Ludwig Wittgenstein for Solution-Focused Brief Therapy?* Available online at www.brief-therapy.org/ steve_thoughts.htm. (accessed online 27 January 2006).

Dhami, M.K. and Joy, P. (2007) Challenges to establishing volunteer run community-based restorative justice programs, *Contemporary Justice Review*, 10: 9–22.

Dhami, M.K., Mantle, G. and Fox, D. (2009) Restorative justice in prisons, *Contemporary Justice Review*, 12(4): 433–48. *Academic Search Premier*, EBSCOhost (accessed 21 December 2009).

Dignan, J. (2003) Towards a systemic model of restorative justice, in A. von Hirsch, J. Roberts, A.E. Bottoms, K. Roach and M. Schiff (eds) *Restorative Justice and Criminal Justice: Competing or Reconcilable Paradigms?* (pp. 135–56). Oxford: Hart Publishing.

Directgov Anti Social Behavior (2012). Available online at www.direct.gov.uk/en/ crimejusticeandthelaw/crimeprevention/dg_4001652 (accessed 23 July 2012).

Dominelli, L. (2002) *Anti-oppressive Social Work Theory and Practice*. Basingstoke: Palgrave Macmillan.

Dugmore, P. and Pickford, S. with Angus, S. (2007) *Youth Justice and Social Work*. Exeter: Learning Matters.

Eitzen, D.S. and Maxine B. (1986) *Social Problems* (3rd edn). Boston, MA: Allyn & Bacon.

Essex County Council (2004) *Family Group Conference*. Available online at www.essexcc.gov. uk/vip8/ecc/ECCWebsite/display/guides/family_group_conferences_guide_262014_ ServicesForChildrenAndYoungPeople/index.jsp (accessed 4 May 2004).

Evans, T. and Harris, J. (2004) Street-level bureaucracy, social work and the (exaggerated) death of discretion, *British Journal of Social Work*, 34: 871–95.

Family Rights Group (2003) *Family Group Conferences*. Available online at www.frg.org.uk/ index.asp (accessed 4 May 2004).

Family Rights Group (2007) *What is a Family Group Conference*. Available online at www.frg. org.uk/fgc_introduction.html (accessed 14 August 2007).

Farrington, D.P. (1984) England and Wales, in M. Klein (ed.) *Western Systems of Juvenile Justice*. Beverly Hills, CA: Sage Publications.

Farrington, D.P. (1996) *Understanding and Preventing Youth Crime.* York: Joseph Rowntree Foundation/York Publishing Services (accessed June 2011).

Farrington, D.P. (1999) Predicting persistent young offenders, in G.L. McDowell and J.S. Smith (eds) *Juvenile Delinquency in the United States and the United Kingdom* (pp. 3–21). London: Macmillan.

Farrington, D.P. (2000) Explaining and preventing crime: the globalization of knowledge. The American Society of Criminology 1999 presidential address, *Criminology*, 38(1): 1–24.

Farrington, D.P. (2001) Key results from the first forty years of the Cambridge study in delinquent development, in T.P. Thornberry and M.D. Krohn (eds) *Taking Stock of Delinquency: An Overview of Findings from Contemporary Longitudinal Studies.* New York: Kluwer/Plenum.

Farrington, D.P. (2002) Developmental criminology and risk focussed prevention, in M. Maguire, R. Morgan and R. Reiner (eds) *The Oxford Handbook of Criminology.* Oxford: Oxford University Press.

Feeley, M.M. and Simon, J. (1996) The new penology, in J. Muncie, E. McLaughlin and M. Langan (eds) *Criminological Perspectives: A Reader* (pp. 367–79). London: Sage Publications.

Feilzer, M. and Hood, R. (2004) *Differences or Discrimination.* London: Youth Justice Board for England and Wales.

Fineberg, A. (2012) Troubled families and local services. Available online at www.guardian. co.uk/guardian-professional (accessed 12 July 2012).

Flood-Page, C., Campbell, S., Harrington, V. and Miller, J. (2000) *Youth Crime: Findings from the 1998/1999 Youth Lifestyles Survey.* Research Study 209. London: Home Office.

Fox, D. (2005) *An Examination of the Implementation of Restorative Justice in Canada, and Family Group Conferencing Approaches in the UK.* Monograph Series. London: BASW/Venture Press.

Fox, D. (2008) Family group conferencing and evidence-based practice: what works? *Research, Policy and Planning,* 26(3): 157–67.

Fox, D., Mantle, G. and Dhami, M.K. (2006) Restorative final warnings: policy and practice, *Howard Journal of Criminal Justice,* 45(2): 129–40.

Freire, P. (1972) *Pedagogy of the Oppressed.* London: Sheed & Ward.

Fullwood, C. and Powell, H. (2004) Towards effective practice in the youth justice system in R. Burnett and C. Roberts (eds) *What Works in Probation and Youth Justice: Developing Evidence-Based Practice.* (pp. 29–45) Portland, OR: Willan.

Fyson, R. and Yates, J. (2011) Anti-social behaviour orders and young people with learning disabilities, *Critical Social Policy,* 31: 102–25.

Garside, R. (2009) *Risky People or Risky Societies? Rethinking Interventions for Young Adults in Transition.* London: Centre for Crime and Justice Studies.

Gavrielides, T. (2003) *Restorative Justice Theory and Practice: Mind the Gap!* Available online at www.restorativejustice.org/rj3/feature/2003/December/RJTheory%26practice.htm (accessed 24 May 2005).

Geese Theatre Company UK (2012) Available online at www.geese.co.uk/

General Social Care Council (GSCC) (2008) *Code of Practice for Social Care Workers and Code of Practice for Employers of Social Care Workers.* Available online at www.gscc.org.uk/NR/rdonlyres/8E693C62-9B17-48E1-A806-3F6F280354FD/0/CodesofPractice.doc (accessed 15 January 2008).

General Social Care Council (GSCC) (2011) *Code of Conduct.* Available online at www.gscc. org.uk/cmsFiles/Registration/Codes%20of%20Practice/Codes_of_PracticeWord_version. doc (accessed 22 August 2011).

Giddens, A. (ed.) (2001) *The Global Third Way Debate*. Oxford: Polity Press.

Glendinning, C., Powell, M. and Rummery, K. (eds) (2002) *Partnership, New Labour and the Governance of Welfare*. Bristol: Policy Press.

Goffman, E. (1959) *The Presentation of Self in Everyday Life*. New York: Anchor Books.

Goldson, B. (2002) New punitiveness: the politics of child incarceration, in J. Muncie, G. Hughes and E. McLaughlin (eds) *Youth Justice: Critical Readings* (pp. 386–400). London : Sage Publications.

Goldson, B. (2005) Child imprisonment: a case for abolition, *Youth Justice*, 5(2): 77–90.

Goldson, B. (2006) Penal custody: intolerance, irrationality and indifference, in B. Goldson and J. Muncie (eds) *Youth Crime and Justice* (pp. 139–56). London: Sage Publications.

Goldson, B. and Coles, D. (2008) Child deaths in the juvenile secure estate, in M. Blyth, C. Wright and R. Newman (eds) *Children and Young People in Custody*. Bristol: Policy Press.

Goldson, B. and Muncie, J. (eds) (2008) *Youth Crime and Justice*. London: Sage Publications.

Graef, R. (2000) *Why Restorative Justice? Repairing the Harm Caused by Crime*. London: Calouste Gulbenkian Foundation.

Gray, I., Parker, J., Rutter, L. and Williams, S. (2010) Developing communities of practice: a strategy for effective leadership, management and supervision in social work, *Social Work and Social Sciences Review*, 14(2): 20–36.

Guardian, the (2012) *Antisocial Behaviour: Crackdown – and Backdown*. Available online at guardian.co.uk, Tuesday 22 May 2012 (accessed 23 July 2012).

Hagell, A. (2002) *The Mental Health of Young Offenders. Bright Futures: Working with Vulnerable Young People*. London: Mental Health Foundation.

Haines, K. and Case, S. (2008) The rhetoric and reality of the 'risk factor prevention paradigm' approach to preventing and reducing youth offending, *Youth Justice*, 1: 5–20.

Harris, M.K. (1998) Reflections of a sceptical dreamer: some dilemmas in restorative justice theory and practice, *Contemporary Justice Review*, 1(1): 57–69.

Harris, R. and Webb, D. (1987) *Welfare, Power and Juvenile Justice*. London: Tavistock.

Higher Education Academy (2010) *The Role of Youth Courts*. Available online at www.heacademy.ac.uk/home (accessed 9 September 2011).

HM Government (1999) *Modernising Government*. (Cmd 4310) London: HMSO.

HM Government (2003) *Criminal Justice Act 2003*. Available online at www.cps.gov.uk > Legal Resources > Legal Guidance (accessed 21 July 2011).

HM Government (2004) *Every Child Matters Green Paper*. London: HMSO.

HM Government (2011) *Building Engagement, Building Futures: Our Strategy to Maximise the Participation of 16–24 Year Olds in Education, Training and Work*. London: HMSO.

HM Government (2012) *Positive for Youth: A New Approach to Cross-government Policy for Young People aged 13 to 19*. London: HMSO.

Hoge, R.D., Andrews, D.A. and Leschied, A.W. (1994) Test of three hypotheses regarding the predictors of delinquency, *Journal of Abnormal Child Psychology*, 22(5): 547–59.

Home Office (2003) *Restorative Justice: The Government's Strategy. A consultation Document on the Government's Strategy on Restorative Justice 22nd July, 2003*. London: Home Office Communication Directorate.

Hornby, N. (2003) *What is Social Work? Contexts and Perspectives*. Exeter: Learning Matters.

House of Commons Education and Skills Committee (2005) *Prison Education Seventh Report of Session 2004–2005, Volume 1*. Available online at www.publications.parliament.uk/pa/cm200405/cmselect/cmeduski/114/114i.pdf

House of Commons Home Affairs Committee (2007) *Young Black People and the Criminal Justice System. Second Report of Session 2006–2007, Volume 1*. London: The Stationery Office.

Hoyle, C. (2008) *Leading Edge. Restorative Justice*, online at www.restorativejustice.org/leading/hoylecarolyn/

Hoyle, C., Young, R. and Hill, R. (2002) *Proceed With Caution: An Evaluation of the Thames Valley Police Initiative in Restorative Cautioning*. York: Joseph Rowntree Foundation.

Hughes, J. (2005) Doing the arts justice: a review of research literature, practice and theory, in A. Miles and A. Mclewin (eds) *Unit for Arts and Offenders and Centre for Applied Theatre Research*. Accessed online via the IFACCA (International Federation of Arts Councils and Culture Agencies) website at www.ifacca.org/publications/2005/01/01/doing-the-arts-justice-a-review/

Hugman, R. (1991) *Power in the Caring Professions*. Houndmills: Macmillan.

Ife, J. (2002) *Community Development: Community-based Alternatives in an Age of Globalisation* (2nd edn). Frenchs Forest, Australia: Longman.

IYO/CJJI (HMI Probation, the Care Quality Commission, Estyn, Healthcare Inspectorate Wales and Ofsted) (2011) *To Get the Best Results: A Joint Inspection of Offending Behaviour, Health and Education, Training & Employment Interventions in Youth Offending Work in England ad Wales*. London: HMSO. London.

James, A., Jenks, C. and Prout, A. (1998) *Theorizing Childhood*. Cambridge: Polity Press.

Jermyn, H. (2001) *The Arts and Social Exclusion: A Review prepared for the Arts Council of England*, accessed online via the Arts Council of England website at www.artscouncil.org.uk/publication_archive/arts-and-social-exclusion-a-review-prepared-for-the-arts-council-of-england/

Johns, R.G. (2007) *Using the Law in Social Work* (3rd edn). Exeter: Learning Matters.

Johnstone, G. (2002) *Restorative Justice Ideas, Values, Debates*. Cullompton: Willan Publishing.

Jordan, B. (1998) *The New Politics of Welfare: Social Justice in a Global Context*. London: Sage Publications.

Juby, H. and Farrington, D.P. (2001) Disentangling the link between disrupted families and delinquency, *British Journal of Criminology*, 41: 22–40.

Keating, M. (2002) American sociology and the interactive self, in I. Marsh (ed.) *Theory and Practice in Sociology* (pp. 180–217). Harlow: Pearson Education.

Khan, L. (2010) *Reaching Out, Reaching In: Promoting Mental Health and Emotional Well-being in Secure Settings*. London: Centre for Mental Health.

King, M. and Piper, C. (1995) *How the Law Thinks About Children*. Aldershot: Arena.

Klein, M. (1984) *Western Systems of Juvenile Justice*. Beverly Hills, CA: Sage Publications.

Lader, D., Singleton, N. and Meltzer, H. (2000) *Psychiatric Morbidity among Young Offenders in England and Wales*. London: Office for National Statistics (ONS).

Latimer, J., Dowden, C. and Muise, D. (2001) *The Effectiveness of Restorative Justice Practices: A Meta-analysis*. Ottawa: Research and Statistics Division, Department of Justice.

Lemonne, A. (2003) Alternative conflict resolution and restorative justice: a discussion, in L. Walgrave (ed.) *Repositioning Restorative Justice* (pp. 43–65). Devon: Willan Publishing.

Liddle, M. (2008) *Wasted Lives: Counting the Cost of Juvenile Offending*. London: NACRO.

Liebman, M. (2007) *Restorative Justice: How it Works*. London: Jessica Kingsley Publishers.

Lipsky, M. (1983) *Street Level Bureaucracy*. London: Russell Sage Foundation.

Lishman, J. (2009) *Communication in Social Work*. London: Palgrave Macmillan.

Littlechild, B. and Smith, R. (2008) Social work with young offenders, in K. Wilson, G. Ruch, M. Lymbery and A. Cooper (eds) *Social Work: An Introduction to Contemporary Practice*. Harlow: Pearson Education.

Llewellyn, A., Agu, L. and Mercer, D. (2008) *Sociology for Social Workers*. Cambridge: Polity Press.

Llewellyn, K. and Hoebel, A. (1941) The Cheyenne way, in K. Roach (2000) Changing punishment at the turn of the century: restorative justice on the rise, *Canadian Journal of Criminology*, 42(3):249–81.

Lupton, C. and Stevens, M. (1997) *Family Outcomes: Following Through on Family Group Conferences*. Portsmouth: Social Services and Information Unit, University of Portsmouth.

Lupton, C. and Stevens, M. (2003) Family outcomes: following through on family group conferences, *Protecting Children*, 18(1/2): 127–8.

Mantle, G., Fox, D. and Dhami, M.K. (2005) Restorative justice and three individual theories of crime: *Internet Journal of Criminology*, 1–36. Available online at www.internetjournalofcriminology.com

Marshall, T. (1996) Criminal mediation in Great Britain, *European Journal of Criminal Policy and Research*, 4(4): 21–43.

Mason, P. and Prior, D. (2008) *Engaging Young People Who Offend*. London: Youth Justice Board.

Mathews, R. and Young, J. (eds) (2003) *The New Politics of Crime and Punishment*. Devon: Willan Publishing.

McCold, P. (1999) *Restorative Justice Practice: The State of the Field*, International Institute for Restorative Practices, Community Service Foundation, Pipersville, PA.

McCold, P. and Wachtel, T. (2004) In pursuit of paradigm: a theory of restorative justice. Available online at www.restorativepractices.org/library/paradigm.html (accessed 5 March 2004).

Merkel-Holguin, L. (1996) *Putting Families Back into the Child Protection Partnership: Family Group Decision Making*. Available online at www.americanhumane.org/site/PageServer?pagename_pc_fgdm_what_is (accessed 1 September 2008).

Merkel-Holguin, L., Nixon, P. and Burford, G. (2003) Learning with families: a synopsis of FGDM research and evaluation in child welfare, *Protecting Children*, 18(1/2): 2–11.

Miers, D. (2001) *An International Review of Restorative Justice*. Crime Reduction Series Paper 10. London: Home Office.

Milner, J. and O'Byrne, P. (2009) *Assessment in Social Work* (3rd edn). Basingstoke: Palgrave Macmillan.

Ministry of Justice (2008) *Delivering Every Child Matters in Secure Settings: A Practical Toolkit for Improving the Health and Well-being of Young People*. Available online at www.justice.gov.uk/downloads/youth-justice/custody/hein_toolkit_final.pdf/

Ministry of Justice (2010) *Breaking the Cycle: Government Response: 1*. London: Crown Copyright 2010.

Ministry of Justice (2011) *Youth Justice Statistics 2009/10 England and Wales*. Available online at www.justice.gov.uk/downloads/publications/statistics-and-data/mojstats/yjb-annual-workload-data-0910.pdf (accessed 20 June 2011).

Ministry of Justice (2012) *Summary of Crime and Disorder Act 1998 – Statutory Functions of a YOT*. Available outline at www.justice.gov.uk/youth-justice/courts-and-orders/youth-offending-teams/summary-of-crime-and-disorder-act-1998-statutory-functions-of-a-yot

Mirsky, L. (2003) *Family Group Conferencing Worldwide: Part 1 in a Series*. Available online at www.iirp.org/pages/fgcseries01.html (accessed 26 January 2006).

Moffat, K. (1996) Teaching social work as a reflective process, in N. Gould and I. Taylor (eds) *Reflective Learning for Social Work*. Aldershot: Arena/Gower.

MORI (2009) *Youth Survey 2008: Young People in Mainstream Education*. London: YJB.

Morris, A. (2002) Critiquing the critics: a brief response to critics of restorative justice. *British Journal of Criminology*, 42(3): 596–615. Oxford: Oxford University Press.

Morris, K. and Sheperd, C. (2000) Family involvement in child protection: the use of family group conferences, in H. Kemshall and R. Littlechild (eds) *User Involvement and Participation in Social Care: Research Informing Practice*. London: Jessica Kingsley Publishers.

Mullaly, B. (2007) *The New Structural Social Work*. Canada: Oxford University Press.

Muncie, J. (2009) *Youth Crime* (3rd edn). London: Sage Publications.

Munro, E. (2011) *The Munro Review of Child Protection: Final Report. A Child-centred System*. Available online at www.education.gov.uk/munroreview/downloads/8875_DfE_Munro_Report_TAGGED.pdf (accessed 12 June 2012).

Mutter, R., Shemmings, D., Dugmore, P. and Hyare, M. (2008) Family group conferences in youth justice, *Health and Social Care in the Community*, 16(3): 262–70.

O'Connell, T. (1998) From Wagga Wagga to Minnesota. Paper presented at *Conferencing: A New Response to Wrongdoing. Proceedings of the First North American Conference on Conferencing*, Bethlehem, PA: Real Justice.

O'Connell, T., Wachtel, B. and Wachtel, T. (1999) *Conferencing Handbook: The New Real Justice Training Manual*. Pipersville, PA: The Piper's Press.

O'Hagan, K. (2006) *Identifying Emotional and Psychological Abuse: A Guide for Childcare Professionals*. New York: Open University Press.

O'Neill, A. and Heaney, M. (2000) Restored or 'restoried': a consideration of the links between systemic family therapy and restorative justice, *Child Care in Practice*, 6(4): 368–9.

Parliament UK (2010) *Prison Population Statistics December 2010*. Available online at www.parliament.uk/briefingpapers/commons/lib/research/briefings/snsg-04334.pdf (accessed 20 June 11).

Parr, S. (2011) Family, policy and the governance of anti-social behaviour in the UK: women's experiences of intensive family support, *Journal of Social Policy*, 40(4): 717–37.

Payne, M. (2005) *Modern Social Work Theory* (3rd edn). Basingstoke: Macmillan.

Phillips, A., Powell, H., Anderson, F. and Popiel, A. (2009) *Youth Survey 2008: Young People in Mainstream Education*. London: Youth Justice Board. Available online at www.yjb.gov.uk/publications/ Resources/Downloads/MORI_08_fullreport_EDU.pdf

Pickford, J. (2000) *Youth Justice: Theory and Practice*. London: Cavendish.

Pickford, J. and Dugmore, P. (2012) *Youth Justice and Social Work*. London: Sage Learning Matters.

Pitts, J. (1990) *Working With Young Offenders*. Basingstoke: Macmillan.

Pranis, K. (2000) Conferencing and the community, in G. Burford and J. Hudson (eds) *Family Group Conferencing* (pp. 40–49). New York: Walter de Gruyeter, Inc.

Preston-Shoot, M. and Agass, D. (1990) *Making Sense of Social Work: Psychodynamics, Systems and Practice*. Basingstoke: Macmillan.

Prior, D. (2009) The 'problem' of anti-social behaviour and the policy knowledge base: analysing the power/knowledge relationship, *Critical Social Policy*, 29: 5–23.

Prison Reform Trust (2007) Criminal damage: Why We Should Lock Up Fewer Children. A Prison Reform Trust briefing. Available online at www.prisonreformtrust.org.uk/Portals/0/Documents/criminal%20damge%20-%20why%20we%20should%20lock%20up%20fewer%20children.pdf (accessed 10 June 2011).

Raynor, P. and Lewis, S. (2011) Risk–need assessment, sentencing and minority ethnic offenders in Britain, *British Journal of Social Work*, 41: 1357–71.

Rees, S. and Wallace, A. (1982) *Verdicts on Social Work*. London: Edward Arnold.

Restorative Justice Consortium (2011) *Principles of Restorative Justice*. Available online at www.restorativejustice.org.uk/resources/pdf/Principles_final_doc_2006.pdf (accessed 22 November 2007).

Restorative Justice Oak Bay (2003) Facilitator training leaflet, 21–23 February.

Richards, S., Ruch, G. and Trevithick, P. (2005) Communication skills training for practice: the ethical dilemma for social work education, *Social Work Education: The International Journal*, 24(4): 409–22.

Roach, K. (2000) Changing punishment at the turn of the century: restorative justice on the rise, *Canadian Journal of Criminology*, 42(3): 249–81.

Roberts P. (2006) *Penal Offence in Question: Some Reference Points for Interdisciplinary Conversation*, in A.V. Hirsch and A.P. Simester (eds) *Incivilities: Regulating Offensive Behaviour*. Oxford: Hart Publishing.

Ronen, T. (1997) Cognitive-behavioural therapy, in M. Davis (ed.) *The Blackwell Companion to Social Work* (pp. 202–13). Oxford: Blackwell Publishers

Rutter, M. (1987) Psychosocial resilience and protective mechanisms, *American Journal of Orthopsychiatry*, 57(3): 316–31.

Sackett, D.L., Rosenberg, W.M., Gray, J.A., Haynes, R.B. and Richardson, W.S. (1996) Evidence based medicine: what it is and what it isn't, *British Medical Journal* 312(7023): 71–2.

Saenz de Ugarte, L. and Martin-Aranaga, I. (2012) Social work and risk society: the need for shared social responsibility, *European Journal of Social Work*, 14(4): 447–62.

Sarnoff, S. (2001) Restoring justice to the community: a realistic goal, *Federal Probation*, 651: 33–9.

Schon, D. (1983) *The Reflective Practitioner: How Professionals Think in Action*. New York: Basic Books.

Scottish Institute for Excellence in Social Work Education and Social Care Institute for Excellence (SCIE) *Evaluating Outcomes in Social Work Education*. London: SCIE. Available online at www.scie.org.uk (accessed 21 October 2012).

Seymour, C. and Seymour, R. (2007) *Court Room Skills for Social Workers*. Exeter: Learning Matters.

Shapland, J., Atkinson, A., Colledge, E., Dignan, J., Howes, M., Johnstone, J., Pennant, R., Robinson, G. and Sorsby, A. (2004) *Implementing Restorative Justice Schemes (Crime Reduction Programme): A Report on the First Year*, Home Office Online Report 32/04.

Shapland, J., Robinson, G. and Sorsby, A. (2011) *Restorative Justice in Practice*. London: Routledge.

Sharpe, S. (1998) *Restorative Justice: A Vision for Healing and Change*. Edmonton, Canada: Mediation and Restorative Justice Centre.

Shaw, M. and Jane, F. (1999) *Family Group Conferencing with Children Under Twelve: A Discussion Paper*. Ottawa, Canada: Department of Justice.

Sheldon, B. (2001) The validity of evidence-based practice in social work: a reply to Stephen Webb, *British Journal of Social Work*, 31: 801–09.

Shlonsky, A. and Wagner, D. (2005) The next step: integrating actuarial assessment and clinical judgement into an evidence-based practice framework in CPS case management, *Children and Youth Services Review*, 27: 409–27.

Simmonds, J., Bull, H. and Martyn, H. (1998) *Family Group Conferences in Greenwich Social Services*. London: Goldsmith College.

Smith, D. (2004) *Edinburgh Study of Youth Transitions and Crime: The Links between Victimisation and Offending*. Edinburgh: University of Edinburgh.

Smith, D. and McAra, L. (2004) *Gender and Youth Offending*. Edinburgh: Edinburgh University Press.

Smith, D., McVie, S., Woodward, R., Shute, J. and McCara, V. (2001) *Edinburgh Study of Youth Transitions and Crime Key Findings Ages 12 and 13*. Edinburgh: University of Edinburgh.

Smith, L. and Hennessy, J. (1998) *Making a Difference: The Essex Family Group Conference Project*. Chelmsford: Essex Social Services.

Smith, R. (2006) Actuarialism and early intervention in contemporary youth justice in B. Goldson and J. Muncie (eds) *Youth Crime and Justice* (pp. 92–110). London: Sage Publications.

Social Work Reform Board (SWRB) (2010) *Implementing the Recommendations of the Social Work Task Force*. Available online at www.education.gov.uk/swrb (accessed 7 October 2012).

Stahlkopf, C. (2009) Restorative justice, rhetoric, or reality? Conferencing with young offenders, *Contemporary Justice Review*, 12(3): 231–51.

Stanford, S.N. (2011) Constructing moral responses to risk: a framework for hopeful social work practice, *British Journal of Social Work*, 41: 1514–31.

Steffensmeier, D., Schwartz, J., Zhong, H. and Ackerman, J. (2005) An assessment of recent trends in girls' violence using diverse longitudinal sources: is the gender gap closing?, *Criminology*, 43(2): 355–405.

Stenson, K. (1991) The scope of crime and the problems of definition, in K. Stenson and D. Cowell (eds) *The Politics of Crime Control* (pp. 1–32) London: Sage.

Sullivan, D. and Tift, L. (2001) *Restorative Justice: Healing the Foundations of our Everyday Lives*. New York: Willow Tree Press.

Sundell, K. and Vinnerljung, B. (2004) Outcomes of family group conferencing in Sweden: a 3-year follow-up, *Child Abuse and Neglect*, 28(3): 267–87.

Sutherland, A. (2009) The 'scaled approach' in youth justice: fools rush in . . ., *The National Association for Youth Justice*, 9(1): 44–60. London: Sage Publications.

Sutherland, E.H. (1962) Is 'white collar crime' crime?, in M.E. Wolfgand, L.D. Savitz and N.B. Johnston (eds) *White Collar Crime*. New York: Holt, Rinehart & Winson.

Tarling, R. and Adams, M. (2012), *Summer Arts Colleges Digest of the Evaluation Report 2007–2011*. Available online at www.unitas.uk.net/Assets/305157/Document.pdf?1339601384

Taylor, I. (1996) Reflective learning and social work for the twenty-first century, in N., Gould, and I. Taylor (eds) *Reflective Learning for Social Work*. Aldershot: Arena/Gower.

Teli, B. (2011) *Assessment and Planning Interventions: Review and Redesign Project. Statement of Intent – Proposed Framework*. London: YJB.

Terrill, R. (1992) *World Criminal Justice Systems: A Survey*. Cincinnati. OH. Anderson Publishing.

The Children's Society (2011) Well-being, not 'well good', The Good Childhood Blog, 26 April 2011. Available online at www.childrenssociety.org.uk/news-views/good-childhood-blog/well-being-not-well-good (accessed 10 April 2012).

The Children's Society (2012) *Our response to the Riots Communities and Victims Panel*, Press Release, 28 March 2012 all day. Available online at www.childrenssociety.org.uk/news-views/press-release/our-response-riots-communities-and-victims-panel-report (accessed 9 October 2012).

Thompson, N. (2005) *Understanding Social Work: Preparing for Practice*. Basingstoke: Palgrave Macmillan.

Thompson, N. (2006) *Anti Discriminatory Practice: Practical Social Work*. Basingstoke: Macmillan.

Thompson, N. and Thompson, S. (2008) *Social Work Companion*. London: Palgrave Macmillan.

Thurman-Eyer, D. and Mirsky, L. (2009) *Family Group Decision Making Helps Prison Inmates Reintegrate into Society*. Available online at www.iirp.org/familypower/library/fgdm-prisons. html?utm_source=Restorative+Practices+eForumandutm_campaign=2a23034c43-eForum_FGDM_in_Prison9_22_2009&utm_medium=email (accessed 21 September 2009).

TIPP (2012) Available online at www.tipp.org.uk/

Umbreit, M.S. and Coates, R.B. (1999) Multicultural implications of restorative juvenile justice, *Federal Probation*, 63(2): 44–52.

Umbreit, M.S and Zehr, H. (1996) Restorative family group conferences: differing models and guidelines for practice, *Federal Probation*, 60(3): 24–30.

Unitas (2012) Available online at www.unitas.uk.net/SummerArtsColleges/Survey/

United Nations (2002) *Resolution 2002/12: Basic Principles on the Use of Restorative Justice Programmes in Criminal Matters*. Available online at www.asc41.com/un2.htm (accessed 22 May 2005).

Van Ness, D. (1986) *Crime and its Victims*. Downers Grove, IL: Intervarsity Press. In K. Roach, (ed.) (2000) Changing punishment at the turn of the century: restorative justice on the rise, *Canadian Journal of Criminology*, 42(3): 249–80.

van Pagee, R. (2003) cited in L. Mirsky (2003a) *Family Group Conferencing Worldwide: Part 1 in a Series*. Available online at www.iirp.org/pages/fgcseries01.html (accessed 3 April 2003).

Web, S.A. (2001) Some considerations on the validity of evidence based practice in social work, *British Journal of Social Work*, 31: 57–79.

Wilcox, A. and Hoyle, C. (2004) *The National Evaluation of the Youth Justice Board's Restorative Justice Projects*. London: Youth Justice Board for England and Wales.

Wilding, P. (1982) *Professional Power and Social Welfare*. London: Routledge & Kegan Paul.

Wilding, P. and Wardhaugh, J. (1993) Toward an explanation of the corruption of care, *Critical Social Policy*, 131: 4–31.

Wilson, D. and Moore, S. (2004) *Playing the Game: The Experiences of Young Black Men in Custody*. London: The Children's Society.

Wilson, J.Q. and Kelling, G. (1982) Broken windows, *Atlantic Monthly*, March, 29–38.

Wilson, K., Ruch, G., Lymbery, M. and Cooper, A. (2008) *Social Work: An Introduction to Contemporary Practice*. Harlow: Pearson Education.

Wood, M. (2005) *The Victimization of Young People: Findings from the Crime and Justice Survey 2003*, Home Office Research Findings, No. 246. London: Home Office.

World English Dictionary (2011) Available online at www.dictionary.reference.com/browse/victim (accessed 1 July 2011).

Young, R. and Goold, B. (1999) Restorative police cautioning in Aylesbury – from degrading to reintegrative shaming ceremonies?, *Criminal Law Review*, February, 126–38.

Youth Justice Board (YJB) (undated) *Referral Orders: A summary of Research into the Issues Raised in The Introduction of Referral Orders in the Youth Justice System*. Available online at www.yjb.gov.uk/Publications/Resources/Downloads/RefOrdSum.pdf (accessed 12 June 2011).

Youth Justice Board (2000) *Asset: Intervention Plan Guidance*. London: YJB.

Youth Justice Board (2001) *Positive Parenting*. Available online at www.yjb.gov.uk/publications/Resources/Downloads/PosParentSum.pdf (accessed 14 January 2012).

Youth Justice Board (2003) *Referral Order Research into the Issues Raised in the 'Introduction of the Referral Order in the Youth Justice System*. Available online at www.youth-justice-board.gov.uk/Publications/Downloads/Referral%20Orders%20(Full%20Report).pdf (accessed 30 May 2005).

Youth Justice Board (2004) *Differences or Discrimination?* Available online at www.yjb.gov.uk/publications/Resources/Downloads/Differences%20or%20Discrimination%20-%20Summary.pdf (accessed 21 November 2011).

Youth Justice Board (2005) *A Summary of Risk and Protective Factors Associated with Youth Crime and Effective Interventions to Prevent It*, Research Note No. 5. London: YJB.

Youth Justice Board (2007a) *Accommodation Needs and Experiences*. Available online at www.yjb.gov.uk/publications/Resources/Downloads/Accommodation%20Needs%20and%20Experiences%20-%20Summary.pdf (accessed on 10 June 11).

Youth Justice Board (2007b) Summary of 12 Month ISSP. London: YJB.

Youth Justice Board (2008) *Assessment, Planning Interventions and Supervision: A Source Document*. London: YJB.

Youth Justice Board (2009) *Youth Rehabilitation Order with Intensive Supervision and Surveillance (ISS)*. Available online at www.justice.gov.uk/downloads/guidance/youth-justice/reducing-re-offending/YROwithISSOperationalGuidance.pdf (accessed 2 December 2011).

Youth Justice Board (2010a) *National Standards for Youth Justice Services*. Available online at www.yjb.gov.uk/publications/Resources/Downloads/National%20Standards%20for%20 Youth%20Justice%20Services.pdf (accessed 16 January 2012).

Youth Justice Board (2010b) *The Scaled Approach*. Available online at www.yjb.gov.uk/ publications/Resources/Downloads/Youth%20Justice%20the%20Scaled%20 Approach%20-%20A%20framework%20for%20assessment%20and%20interventions.pdf (accessed 21 August 2011).

Youth Justice Board (2010c) *The Art of Engaging Young People*. Available online at www.cjp.org. uk/publications/archive/the-art-of-engaging-young-people-13–09–2010/

Youth Justice Board (2012) *Prevention Brochure (B313)*. Available online at www.yjb.gov.uk/ publications/Resources/Downloads/YJB%20Corporate%20Brochure%20-%20 Prevention%20(English).pdf

Youth Justice Board, Children's Commissioner and User Voice (2011) *Young People's Views on Safeguarding in the Secure Estate: A User Voice Report for the Youth Justice Board and the Office of the Children's Commissioner*. London: YJB.

Youth Justice Briefing (2007) *YJB response to Children in Care Green Paper*. Available online at www.yjb.gov.uk/en-gb/Bulletins/YouthJusticeBriefing/youthjusticebriefing022007.htm (accessed 25 September 2008).

Zehr, H. (1990) *Changing Lenses: A New Focus for Crime and Justice*. Scottsdale, PA: Herald Press.

Zehr, H. (2002) *The Little Book of Restorative Justice*. Intercourse, PA: Good Books.

Zehr, H. and Mika, H. (1998) Fundamental concepts of restorative justice, *Contemporary Justice Review*, 1(1): 47–55.

Zernova, M. (2007) Aspirations of Restorative Justice Proponents and Experiences of Participants in Family Group Conferences, *British Journal of Criminology*, 47: 491–509.

Index